Death under the Shadow of Judiciary

Death under the Shadow of Judiciary

Dr. N.M. Ghatate

Ocean Books Pvt. Ltd.
ISO 9001:2015 Publishers

Published by
Ocean Books (P) Ltd.
4/19 Asaf Ali Road,
New Delhi-110 002 (INDIA)
e-mail: info@oceanbooks.in

ISBN 978-81-8430-348-3
DEATH UNDER THE SHADOW OF JUDICIARY
by Dr. N.M. Ghatate

Edition
2025

Price
₹ 500.00 (Rupees Five Hundred only)

Printed at
Yash Printographics, Noida

Preface

The creation of the United Nations in the backdrop of World War II coupled with the holocaust and genocide of ethnic minorities which claimed millions of lives, respect for human rights and fundamental freedoms, became the anchor of the United Nations. The movement for abolition of death punishment along with world disarmament and a nuclear-free world gathered momentum. With the end of the Cold War followed by the era of economic liberalisation, all-round development and the hope of economic prosperity, it was thought that the abolition of capital punishment would gain worldwide acceptance. However, this was not to be. The expected era of tranquility was threatened by the rise of international terrorism. It first occurred in India in the nineteen eighties and spread to the United States of America and encompassed Europe, parts of Russia and China. It has been basically fuelled by Islamic fundamentalism partly because of economic exploitation of the Islamic world and its intolerance of other faiths. Neither there is the possibility of threat to world peace decreasing nor brutal killing of innocent people without any respect for their human rights.

The net result is that those countries which have retained death punishment are not likely to give it up as long as this threat exists.

Thus, the main focus of this work is to make death punishment as humane as possible in view of advances in technology in execution of death sentence so that the State performs its duty of protecting innocent lives and its integrity without being vengeful or cruel towards the guilty for taking lives of innocent people. The issue of death punishment is inexorably interlinked with and cannot be isolated from the question of extinguishing life, yet an attempt is made to keep the question of death punishment on the periphery as much as possible while dealing with the methods of extinguishing life. To this end, after Introduction — Chapter 1, various modes of death punishment in the Middle Ages and in the present are examined in Chapters 2 and 3. Narratives of some famous and controversial executions along with experiences of the witnesses of executions are also included.

The world situation on death penalty along with the Resolutions of the United Nations and available statistics are given in Chapter 4. The situation in the United States with relevant statistics and recent important judgements of the Supreme Court of United States are included in Chapter 5.

The situation in India is dealt separately. Chapter 6 covers Indian laws and procedures on death punishment with important judgements of the Supreme Court as well as military laws and International Law of War. The procedure for executing death punishment and appellate procedure are given in Chapters 7 and 8. This is followed by public response regarding death punishment and related matters with diagrams in Chapter 9. And the final Chapter 10 contains Conclusion and Recommendations as also problems facing the international community.

On joining the Law Commission of India, I persuaded the Commission to undertake a study in this sphere; the result was the 187th Law Commission Report under the Chairmanship of Justice M. Jagannadha Rao, titled 'Mode of Execution of Death Sentence and Incidental Matters, 2003'. I am indebted to the Law Commission of India for allowing me to use this Report in the preparation of this book.

I especially want to record my sincere thanks to my friend, the late S.V. Deshpande, Advocate of the Supreme Court of India, for assisting me in research regarding methods of death punishment in various countries. I am also grateful to Ms. Khushboo Kataruka for her valuable assistance given during her internship in collecting data with charts, maps, photographs and judgements of foreign countries.

I shall be failing in my duty if I do not record my appreciation to Dr. T.K. Viswanathan, who was Member-Secretary of the Law Commission at that time, and was later the Secretary-General of Lok Sabha, Parliament House, New Delhi, for encouraging me to write this book. I am equally obliged to my son, Vinayak Ghatate, in devoting his time to read the manuscript and make useful suggestions.

I owe debt of gratitud to Gopal Tandon for reading the manuscript of the book and suggeting some editorial changes which have been very helpful in removing errors and improving in text.

I am also thankful to Mr. S.C. Aggarwal and Mr. Abraham Varghese. Both have taken a lot of pain in typing this manuscript and in giving me whatever support I needed.

Needless to say, I take full responsibility for any mistakes of omission and commission.

—Dr. N.M. Ghatate

Contents

List of Illustrations

PICTURES

MAPS

CHARTS

1
Introduction

"State should not punish with vengeance"
—Emperor Ashoka

The twentieth century was a violent century. It witnessed the two World Wars, Korean War, Indo-China War, Vietnam War, the Sino-Indian conflict and two India-Pakistan wars, which resulted in millions of deaths. It was expected that with the end of the cold war and emphasis on economic development the twenty-first century would be one of peace and prosperity; but if the first decade is any indication, this century may not be different than the previous one.

The United Kingdom and democracies of Europe and Latin America have abolished death sentence for the last fifty years. But with the rise of terrorism on the international plane, and murder which particularly in India has targeted innocent lives, the abolition of death punishment is doubtful in the foreseeable future. Recently, Sri Lanka and Pakistan have reinstated the death punishment. Abolitionists argue that it is not a deterrent while the other side argues that those who take innocent lives and who commit pre-meditated cold-blooded murders have no right to live and life-long imprisonment, which involves feeding and clothing them is intolerable as it means spending taxpayers' money. However, the debate on the pros and cons of the death penalty continues. Yet it is losing its edge in India.

This book deals with judicial execution, the methods of death punishment in the past and the present and the situation of death punishment in the world, with emphasis on the two largest democracies — the United States of America and India which have retained death punishment. In the United States of America, the legislatures as well as the courts have played an important role in humanizing methods of capital sentence. However, in India, a century-and-a-half method of hanging by rope till the convict is dead still persists despite the recommendations of two reports of the Law Commission of India, viz. 35th Report titled 'Capital Punishment of 1967' and the 187th Report titled 'Execution of Death Sentence and Incidental Matters, 2003' which looked into various modes of execution of death penalty as prevalent at that time. The 35th Report of the Law Commission concluded, "We find that there is a considerable body of opinion which would like hanging to be replaced by something more humane and more painless." However, the Commission was not able to arrive at any firm conclusion on this point and it observed:

> "The matter is, to a certain extent, one of medical opinion. That a method which is certain, humane, quick and decent should be adopted, is the general view, with which few can quarrel. It is true that the really agonizing part is the anticipation of impending death. But society owes to itself that the agony at the exact point of execution be kept to the minimum. Progress in the science of anesthetics and further study of the various methods, as well as the experience gathered in other countries and development and refinement of the existing methods,

would perhaps, in future, furnish a firm basis for conclusion on this controversial subject. We do not, therefore, recommend a change in the law on this point. We should, however, state here that we do not subscribe to the view that the substitution of any other method will reduce the deterrent effect of the penalty of death."

Earlier, the Royal Commission in its report on Capital Punishment 1949-1953 also dealt with the then prevalent modes of execution of death punishment and stated that three conditions should be fulfilled in executing the death sentence: (a) it should be as less painful as possible; (b) it should be as quick as possible; and (c) there should be least mutilation of the body. It further observed:

"In carrying out this task, the Commission did not confine itself to the four main methods of execution (lethal gas, shooting, electrocution and guillotine). It persuaded enquiry whether there was any method still untried that would inflict death as painless and certain as hanging but with greater decency and without the degrading and barbarous association with which hanging is tainted....

The Commission decided for various reasons that if lethal injection were to be constituted as method of judicial execution in the same case... "The question should be periodically examined especially in light of progress made in the science of anesthetics".

However, in *Bachan Singh's* case, 1980 (2) SCC 684, the Constitutional validity of the death sentence was upheld by the Constitution Bench of the Supreme Court of India by majority of 4:1 with Justice P.N. Bhagwati dissenting. He said, "It cannot be denied that the death punishment is qualitatively different from any other punishment as much as it is irreversible and if an error is committed, there is no way to rectify the error." He also observed that the mode of hanging was inhuman, and barbaric [1983 (3) SCC 24].

The incident which provoked me to write this book has an interesting origin. A poor man who was sentenced to death wrote a post-card with a signed *vakalatnama* (power of attorney) in 1982-83 to Atal Bihari Vajpayee for help. That post-card gave no details except to state that his appeal as well as mercy petition had been dismissed even though the punishment of similarly placed persons in the death-row was commuted to life imprisonment. It was simply signed 'Deena', Meerut Jail, U.P. Mr. Vajpayee who often sent such cases to me, sent Deena's case too to me, asking me to help him if I could.

I made the file but as there was no money in it or any further communication forgot all about it. Many months later, late one night I got a telephone call from Meerut. I was a little surprised as I did not know anyone there. The person ringing me introduced himself as the Superintendent of Meerut Jail and asked if I had the case of Deena. On replying in the affirmative, he asked me about it as his *Kala Warrant* (Death Warrant), fixing the date of execution, had been received. I was shocked and went to my office even though it was late in the night and took out the file. There was nothing in it except two papers.

I wrote a short writ petition with the heading, "Section 353(3) of the Criminal Procedure Code, 1973 which provided for hanging by neck till the person is dead, is unconstitutional and violative of Articles 21 and 19 of the Constitution." In that petition, I briefly narrated that he was a citizen of India and was discriminated as the sentences of some other similarly placed persons had been commuted to life imprisonment, besides adding usual grounds of discrimination and use of archaic methods of extinguishing life as violative of Article 21 of the Constitution of India. While praying for filing a more detailed petition, I asked for stay of execution of the death penalty.

The next day, first thing in the morning, I called my clerk to type out the petition and file it in the Supreme Court. On the opening of the Court at 10.30 a.m., I mentioned the case to the Bench presided by the then Chief Justice of India, Y.V. Chandrachud. He admitted the petition and granted stay of the execution of the death warrant. Subsequently, I filed a detailed petition with a regular affidavit from Deena alias Deena Dayal.

Soon thereafter, Supreme Court closed for the summer vacation. That time several persons, who were facing death sentence including persons like Billa and Ranga of the famous murder case in Delhi, the Abhyankar murder case convicts in Pune and others approached the Supreme Court for stay since they too would have been executed by the same procedure, which was stayed in Deena's case. When one such case came before the vacation judge, Justice Vardarajan, who was a somewhat strict judge, did not believe that this method of punishment which was on the statute book for over hundred years could be challenged and called for Deena's case. On seeing the heading, he granted stay expressing his surprise.

The people of Maharashtra were so exercised over the stay of execution of those convicted for the gruesome murder in the Abhyankar case because of the stay granted by Chief Justice Chandrachud that they cancelled all his social engagements. On the opening of the Court in July 1983 after the summer vacation, a similar case came before Chief Justice Chandrachud. While granting stay, he said he had granted stay because Dr. Ghatate told him his client was over seventy years old and he wished I was present in the Court. After a few days, I had a tenancy case before Chief Justice Chandrachud's court. The first thing he told me was: "Before you argue your case, tell me didn't

I give you stay in that (Deena's) petition because you stated that he was over seventy years old?" I told him I couldn't have because I did not know his age that time and as per the detailed petition filed by me, he was only 48 years old. His annoyance was writ large on his face. He told me that he was fixing the case immediately for final hearing in the next week. Meanwhile, I did extensive research on methods of execution of death punishment, including corresponding with Mr. Bill Dawson, the Senator of the State of Oklahoma in USA which was the first to introduce lethal injection for extinguishing life.

Dena's case [1983 (4) SCC 645] is the only case in India where the constitutionality of the method of execution of death punishment was challenged. This case became famous and was widely covered by the press. But the three-judge Bench of the Supreme Court consisting of Chief Justice Y.V. Chandrachud, Justice R.S. Pathak and Justice Sabhyasachi Mukherjee upheld the validity of Section 354(3) of Criminal Procedure Code, 1973 which provided for hanging by the neck till the person is dead.

Even Mr. Kamal Nath, who was then a Member of Parliament, questioned whether the government was proposing to substitute the matter of hanging by a more humane method such as intravenous injection. Unfortunately, the government replied that it had no such intention.

The author had been concerned about the retention of hanging as the way of extinguishing life and when he joined the Law Commission and was its Vice Chairman. He persuaded the Commission under the Chairmanship of Justice M. Jagannadha Rao to undertake a study on the subject. This resulted in the 187th Report of the Law Commission of India in 2003 titled: Execution of Death Sentence and Incidental Matters. Mr. Arun Jaitley, who was the then Law Minister of India, agreed that the method of execution of death punishment was 'an anarchicism' and the government would give serious thought to implementing the recommendation of the Commission on the mode of imposing death sentence. However, so far death punishment by hanging continues.

India being one of the oldest civilisations in the world owes to itself that the agony at the exact point of execution should be kept to the minimum. This is more so when execution is the result of a judicial verdict. Nor can India shut its eyes to the developments in the execution of death sentence in other parts of the world.

To this end, various modes of execution of death sentence are examined and an attempt is made to suggest reforms needed in the present system of execution of death sentence in India. The purpose of this study is not that death punishment should be abolished or retained but is strictly confined to three issues: (a) the method of execution of death sentence; (b) the process of elimination of differences in judicial opinions among judges of courts in passing sentence of death penalty; and (c) the need to provide a right of appeal to the accused to the Supreme Court in all death sentence matters. In this book, I have referred to the cases decided by the Supreme Court of India, various enactments, and the history of various modes of execution. The situation of death punishment in the world and in the United States of America is examined. Besides various books, articles, newspaper reports, contemporary developments and concerned web articles on these aspects are relied. The questionnaire issued by then Law Commission of India in 2002 which evoked wide public interest is included. Not only did the press give wide publicity but some newspapers and magazines also wrote editorials and articles.

The people, including women, who responded to the questionnaire, came from various walks of life, such as judges, advocates, medical practitioners, armed forces and central police organisations. The responses by e-mail were from India as well as abroad. On the basis of the responses received, statistics were prepared and have been referred to at the end with diagrams.

On the basis of studies and responses, some reforms in the law, which I urgently think are necessary, are also given towards the end.

□

2

Medieval Methods of Execution of Death Punishment[1]

Capital punishment has been in vogue from times immemorial. Various modes and methods of inflicting the death sentence upon a convict as practised in different societies are examined in this chapter. This study is not exhaustive of all the modes of execution but covers some of the important practices followed in the past. In the Middle Ages, death sentence was usually accompanied by cruelty and torture; capital punishment was common for a large number of crimes, including petty offences involving property. In England, during the 18th century, death was the punishment for several specific offences which totalled about a hundred. Death penalty was carried out in various ways. Several methods of execution of death sentences, such as burning at the stake, breaking on the wheel, slow strangulation, crushing under an elephant's feet, throwing from a cliff, boiling in oil, stoning to death and burying alive were practised. Even today, stoning to death is practised in some countries. With the emergence of various principles relating to fair procedure contained in the constitutions of several democratic countries and growth of the human rights movement, such severe death punishments involving torture began to die out since the 18th century. The number of offences punishable by death also reduced in many countries. The idea that punishment by way of death should be swift and humane, whether by hanging, electrocution, gas chamber, shooting or a lethal injection is now followed. Some of the important methods of carrying out the death penalty followed in the past were:

(a) Crucifixion

Fig. Crucifixion of Christ[2]

Nailing a person to a wooden cross and leaving him there till he died was the torturous and popular method of carrying out a death sentence during the years in B.C. Jesus Christ was crucified in this manner. This is the most cruel method of death punishment and reminder of this mode of execution of death punishment is found even today in several countries all over the world in the form of symbol of the cross over every Christian Church.

(b) Burning at the Stake

Fig. Painting by Andyd Share[3]

'Burning' as the method of imposing death punishment dates back to the Christian era. Burning at the stake was a popular form of death sentence and means of torture, which was used mostly for heretics, witches and suspicious women. In the year 643 A.D., an Edict issued by the Pope declared it illegal to burn witches. However, the increased persecution of witches throughout the centuries resulted in millions of women being burned at the stake. The first major witch-hunt occurred in Switzerland in the year 1427 A.D. Throughout the 16th and

17th centuries, witch trials became common throughout Germany, Austria, Switzerland, England, Scotland and Spain during the Inquisition. Soon after, witch trials began to decline in parts of Europe and in England and the death penalty for witches was abolished. The last legal execution by burning at the stake took place at the end of the Spanish Inquisition in 1834.

(c) The Wheel

Fig. Killing Wheel[4]

The wheel as a method of torture and execution was used in a number of ways. A person would be attached to the outer rim of the wheel and then rolled over sharp spikes or down a hill to his death. Also, the wheel could be laid on its side, like a turntable, with the person tied to it. The wheel would turn, and people would take turns beating the victim with iron bars, breaking his bones and eventually causing his death. This method was used throughout Europe, especially during the Middle Ages.

(d) Guillotine

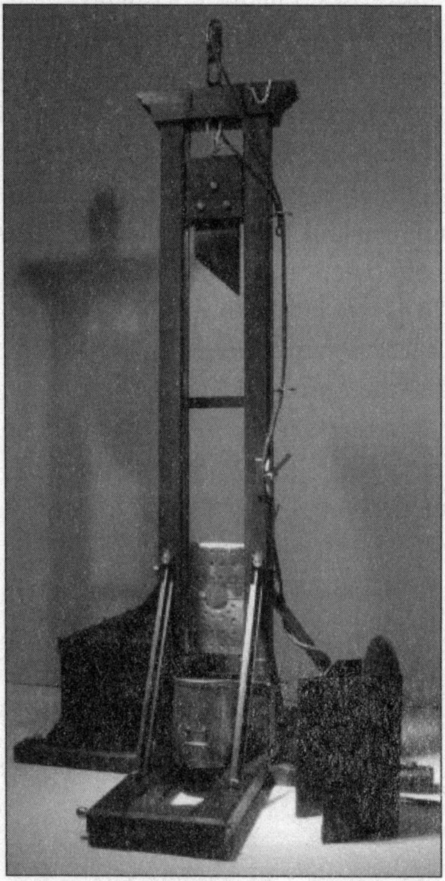

Fig.[5]

Guillotine became a popular form of execution in France in the 1780s. One Dr. Joseph Guillotine proposed that all criminals be executed by the same method so that torture was kept to the minimum. Decapitation was thought to be the least painful and most humane method of execution at that time. Dr. Guillotine suggested that a decapitation machine be built. Subsequently, the decapitation machine came to be named after him. The machine was first tested on sheep and calves, and then on human corpses. Finally, after many improvements and trials, the blade was perfected, and the first execution by guillotine took place in the year 1792. It was widely used during the French Revolution, where many of the executions were held publicly outside the prison of Versailles. The last public execution by guillotine was held in France in June 1939. The last use of guillotine took place in 1977 in France and the device has not officially been used since then. Though guillotine is less painful, it is not acceptable today as it is primitive and involves the mutilation of the condemned person. After France was admitted to the European Union, death sentence itself has been abolished in France.[6]

(e) Headman's Axe

Fig.[7]

This form of execution was quite popular in Germany and England during the 16th and 17th centuries, where decapitation was thought to be the most humane form of capital punishment. An executioner, usually hooded, would chop off the person's head with an axe or sword. The last beheading took place in 1747 in the United Kingdom.[8] Later on, and before capital punishment was abolished recently, with a greater interest in humanitarianism, capital punishment became less gruesome than beheadings and torture that were common place in the earlier centuries. But the practice of beheading for treason existed till 1870.

Story of Beheading of King Charles I
30th January, 1649

Fig. King of England (March 1625 to January 1649)[9]

Charles I was the last absolute monarch of England who believed in the theory of 'Divine Right of the King'. His public execution ended the dynasty of Stuarts.

The affection he showed to his children and the calm courage he displayed on the eve of his execution turned it into a triumph which is still talked about even though three centuries have elapsed since then.

The Trial

After General Oliver Cromwell defeated Charles, he was imprisoned by the Army. In January 1649, General Oliver Cromwell ordered that he be imprisoned at the Cotton Palace in London to 'face the trial', which was to be held at the Westminster Hall. Cromwell constituted a hand-picked tribunal of 135 judges, out of which only 68 turned up for the pre-trial meeting presided by Cromwell. At that meeting, he said that the first question he would ask the tribunal was to show "the authority to try him. We must establish that authority or else we make the King victim and ourselves plain murderers." The trial was to be held to avoid the blame from being called murderers. Yet the tribunal debated about law and the trial procedure for three weeks. The only members who were allowed to attend Parliament were those who Cromwell thought supported the trial. Thus, just 46 Members of Parliament were allowed, out of which 26 voted for the trial. It was called the 'Rump Parliament'. One of the members said, "The king began the Civil War in order to win for himself an unlimited and tyrannical power. He instigated the second conflict which has just been resolved by force of arms. He is guilty on both these charges and the whole is simply this, Sirs, that the king has committed treason against the Realm. What more do we require than that?"

Cromwell who was standing at the window saw a figure surrounded by soldiers. Dressed in elegant velvet black with a wide-rimmed feather hat, the man walked with dignity at an unhurried pace through the icy garden as if he was going to his White Hall Palace till he disappeared in the Cotton Palace. Cromwell trembled at the sight. Turning to the members with a harsh voice, he said, "He comes my friends, he has come. Now we must do that great work. Therefore, we must resolve here and now what the answer we will give the king when he comes before us. Do you know what his first question will be, 'By what authority do you try me? Unless you reply this question, we will have to let him go free.'"

Harry Marten, one of the members of the tribunal, replied, "We try him in name of Parliament and all the good people of England."

Charles was summoned to the Westminster Hall at 1 o'clock in the afternoon for his trial. He took so long to dress that he annoyed his guards. Appearance mattered more to him on that occasion. He wore a black velvet suit with a black silk gown lined with blue satin ribbon and a brilliant Garter with magnificent jewelled St. George and Dragon ornament hung round his neck. The Garter Star was richly embroidered on the back of his gown and his broad black velvet hat with sable plumes. He carried a tall ebony stick with jewelled gold handle and after he had inspected himself, he tapped the stick sharply and gave the order to march forward.

"Hurry, if you please, but take care, you don't come too close, lest you brush against me. I dislike it."

He descended from his sedan chair and hesitated at the threshold of Westminster Hall when Colonel Hacket, an ill-bred officer and chief escort for the journey to London, attempted to take his arm to urge him forward. Charles wrenched his arm away and turned with such expression that the man recoiled. "How dare you put your hand on me? Remember who I am and what you are!"

The Ornate Chair of the Sovereign from which he presided over Parliament was removed. The tribunal sat high and a velvet chair with table were placed lower in front for Charles. Escorting soldiers divided and he marched slowly looking straight as he always did when amongst people. The galleries were packed with soldiers and selected people. As Charles entered the Hall, there was a hushed silence. He did not take off his hat as a mark of respect for the tribunal.

Bradshaw, the President of the court, realising the public anger at the trial and fearing violence wore a metal cap below his hat. He rose nervously and began to read the indictment that Charles was accused of starting the Civil War and instigating the second one. When Bradshaw said that he was "a tyrant and traitor to the Realm", the king, for the first time, looked at the Court and laughed aloud. Bradshaw was so rattled that he stammered over the rest of the charges and finally asked, "What answer do you make to these charges against you?"

The elegant dignified figure in his splendid black with an ancient Royal Order glittering on his breast and shoulders sitting with his legs crossed made the court and spectators which included Cromwell look ridiculous. Addressing the gathering, he spoke slowly:

"If you will tell me what authority I sit here, I shall be willing to answer you. But first, remember," Charles' voice rang out, "I am your King, and the sins you bring upon your heads and the judgement of God upon this land. Think well on it before you go further from one sin to a greater, and tell me by what lawful authority I am seated here. Then I will answer you. But in the meantime, I will not betray my trust. I have a trust committed to me, by God and by ancient lawful descent. I will not betray to answer something unlawful."

Hearing his words, Cromwell mustered, "I know he would refuse to answer it," and asked the tribunal to proceed without it. "It does not matter what he says. The court will find him guilty," Cromwell said.

Bradshaw spoke up as soon as the king had concluded his answer. He was irritated by the king's reply and blurted, "By the authority of the people of England by whom you were elected king."

With a note of mockery in his voice, Charles replied, "No Sir, I deny that. This is not an elective but a hereditary Kingship for these last thousand years. That answer will not do at all. I stand more for liberty of my people than any here who pretend to be my judges."

Without seeming to watch them, Charles saw that hurried conference of judges and his principal enemy Cromwell. 'The Court is adjourned,' Bradshaw called out and pointing a finger at Charles he said, "You are hereby summoned to meet at this place tomorrow at the same hour for the continuance of the trial. I would advice you, Sir, to change your mind and plead when you appear again."

The king stood and ignoring the President he directed his reply at Cromwell in the back row.

"You may bring me here, but a king cannot be tried by any superior power on earth. Produce that power, and I will answer you." And left the Westminster Hall with slow dignified steps with his head held high.

That evening, Cromwell told the judges to proceed with the evidence without Charles' answer to the charges. For the next three days, evidence was recorded which briefly was that the king raised his Royal Standard in the Nottingham war.

Leading the loyalist army, he was himself present at various battlefronts and so on but no witness spoke of his cruelty. The king sat through the proceedings with bored resignation. He was not distressed by anything except the ordeal of walking through the lines of jeering soldiers. Only on the first occasion when they began to shout insults at him did he flush and half turned, but then quickly collected himself and walked as if he had not noticed them.

On the afternoon of January 27, 1949, the Hall seemed to be oppressively quiet, Charles glanced around and saw there were more soldiers present than before and as he sat on his chair. Several of those on the judicial bench avoided looking at him.

After the evidence was over and speeches were made, Bradshaw gathered his papers together; Charles knew he was about to pronounce his sentence and before he could do so, he stood up. He was determined to fight the verdict in the name of the sovereign power he represented personally, though he had little inclination to live when the future at best could hold but a life imprisonment and lasting separation from his family he loved.

"One word before you speak, Sir. A hasty sentence may be repeated, but never be recalled. Before you do this thing, I ask that Commons and Lords may be assembled and I will speak before them both. I abjure you to allow this if as you pretend you value the liberty and peace of this kingdom."

There was a sudden movement among the judges. Colonel Downs, a veteran of the Civil War, was a man of staunch principles. His conscious had been outraged everyday in the Hall. Turning to Bradshaw, he said, "I am not satisfied with this sentence. I cannot give my consent to it." Looking directly at the king, he said, "I want adjournment."

Cromwell rose from his seat and said, "Very well then." He asked Bradshaw to adjourn the court for half-an-hour "while we hear this gentleman".

Charles was removed to an ante-room to wait. His loyal valet Parry came forward with a cup of wine, and went down on his knees before him. Charles took it and thanked him, "Get up, my good Parry. Do not kneel here or you will offend these people."

"Sir, I will kneel to you so long as God gives me the strength to bend my knee," Parry answered. "May I ask you a question?"

"You may, gladly," Charles replied gently.

"What is happening in that place? Why have you come here to wait, Sir?"

"The court, or whatever it calls itself, has been adjourned." Some poor fellow's conscience troubled him and he spoke in my favour. But it will not come to anything. He will either be arrested or he will do what he is told like the rest," Charles said, adding, "It is the rule of history there cannot be two kings in one kingdom. Have no fear for me, for I have none for myself."

Within half-an-hour, Colonel Hacket came and said, "The court has reassembled and Charles Stuart's presence is required."

When Charles was seated, Bradshaw pronounced the verdict: "In the name of Commons and the people of England, Charles is a traitor, tyrant, murderer for all those who died in war and he is sentenced to be beheaded. The court is adjourned."

When Charles came out of the Westminster, soldiers crowded around him and jeered, "Execution, Execution for the tyrant." One Colonel John Hewson elbowed his way and came close up to him. His eyes were blazing with hatred. He had watched Charles deriding the court. He saw him preserving his dignity which was too much for him. He came within a foot of Charles and spat into his face.

The king's expression did not alter. He took out his handkerchief and wiped the spittle from his face and forehead.

"Now tyrant pays for your crimes." Howson hissed at him. Charles gently said, "God has justice in store for you as well as for me."

As he stepped into the sedan chair which he had brought from Cotton House, Charles saw most of the silent crowed massed in the streets and gateway of Westminster fall on their knees with many of them weeping.

When Hacket opened the sedan door and curtly asked him to get in, he showed no trace of anything but dignified indifference.

'Thank God,' Charles remarked as if he was making a conversation, "I shall not have to go to that wretched place again."

After the pronouncement of the verdict, Cromwell sent Charles to sleep at St. James Palace for his last two nights on earth wishing to spare him the sound of incessant hammering of the scaffold that was being prepared for his execution. He allowed former Bishop of London Edward Juxon to bring Charles the consolations of the Anglican religion. The guards were told to stay outside his bedroom. For Charles, it was a blessed interval of peace free of attention of his tormentors. Charles was weary, yet his spirits were high with a strange cheerfulness. He was resigned. There was no sign of despair or even of recrimination. He confessed to priest Juxon that he was happy and ready to exchange the crown torn from him by men for the crown of eternal peace.

Last Meeting with Children

And on the night of Monday, January 29, before he was to die, Cromwell, who was himself a good father, allowed him to meet two of his children, Princess Elizabeth and Prince Henry, as the eldest Prince James had escaped to France and was safe along with his mother Queen Henrietta.

Charles had been waiting impatiently by the window, but it was too dark to see them arrive. When he heard the sound of steps outside his room, some of them light and quick, he turned quickly to Juxon who was standing at the side of the room.

"Pray that I don't break down before them! Whatever their last memory of me, it must be one of courage!"

'It will be, Sir,' the Bishop answered. "Prepare yourself; they're in the ante-chamber."

They came into the room alone, the little Princess Elizabeth, aged thirteen, holding her nine-year-old brother Prince Henry by the hand, and they hesitated, staring at their father as if he were a stranger. It was nearly two years since they had seen him last. Charles walked towards them slowly, and bending down he took his daughter in his arms. He felt the child stiffen as if she were going to pull back, and then suddenly she threw her arms around his neck.

The little Prince came clamouring to be kissed and embraced him with his sister, and for some moments, Charles knelt and held them to him, and the Bishop moved to the door and slipped out, leaving them alone.

"Elizabeth, come, let me look at you — and Henry you too. How big you have both grown! Why, my son, you're quite the man," he said gently, stroking the little boy's head. "Come and sit down with me, here."

They went with him to the fireplace, where a heap of logs was burning brightly. Charles lifted the boy to his knee and held his daughter close to him, his arm round her waist, hers round his neck.

'My children,' he said at last, "my dear children, now I am truly happy."

Elizabeth's eyes were big and blue, very much like his own; there was a shade of red in her brown hair. 'You are a true Stuart,' he told her proudly. "And you, my little son. You are of the Blood Royal, and that is why I must speak to you, not just as your Papa who loves you, but as the King to a Prince and Princess of England. Come closer still, Elizabeth, and listen to what I tell your brother. When I am gone, you must remind him of it at all times."

The firelight blazed and flickered on the small face turned up to him, its forehead shadowed by long curling locks of hair. It was the face of a puzzled little boy who had to be made to understand death and the rights of succession to a Crown. Charles bent down and kissed him on the forehead and then began to speak very quietly.

"Sweetheart, they are going to cut-off your father's head." The boy's eyes opened but he did not speak. "They are going to cut-off my head," Charles repeated slowly. "Mark, my child what I am saying; they will cut-off my head and afterwards they'll try to make you king. But remember this; you must not be a king so long as your brother James is alive. Do you understand sweet one? You must never let them make you king. Give me your promise."

The little Prince's frightened eyes began to fill and then to overflow with tears. He put his knuckles to his mouth and bit them, gazing at the gentle, serious face above him.

"You must not be the king, my son," Charles prompted him, and the child choked through his tears and promised. "I will be torn to pieces first, Papa."

"You are my son and a brave and good boy," Charles whispered to him. "Hold fast to me now, and do not cry. Elizabeth, my daughter, now I must speak to you.

"Tell me what you want me to do," the little girl begged him. She leaned her head against his shoulder. "I will do anything you say, Papa."

"First, I want you to promise not to grieve for me," Charles said. "I shall die a glorious death, my child, remember that. I shall die for the liberty of my people and their ancient laws and for the truth of our religion. You must never forget these things or be tormented by what happens to me. I repeat it again, sweetheart. It will be a glorious death and I am ready for it. Your father is not afraid, nor must you be."

"No Papa, I'm not afraid, I promise you."

"And you must forgive my enemies as I have forgiven them," he said. "That is God's commandment and we must obey it. Never forswear your faith my child; guard it jealously and live by it always."

"I will, Papa, and I will see that Henry does so too."

"Take care of Henry," Charles told her, and taking her hand, he placed it in her brother's. "Hold fast to each other after I am gone, and never forget what I have told you. And give this message to your mother. Elizabeth, whenever God pleases to reunite her and you can tell her in your own words. Tell her," he said slowly — and for a few seconds, he was far away from them, back in White Hall in the happy, vanished past — "tell her that my thoughts have never left her for a moment, and that my love for her will be the same to the last day of my life."

Then there was silence; he sat with his son gathered into his arm, the child's face hidden against his coat. The little Prince was too tired and overwhelmed to cry and he held on to his father as if he would never let him go. The Princess Elizabeth moved and climbed on to his knee and they sat, all three together, without speaking for some moments.

At last, very gently, Charles set them down.

"On that table, there's a box," he said. "Come with me and we will open it. I have a few gifts for you."

To the Bishop he had shown some signs of distress the previous evening because he had nothing to distribute to those who had served him. Money and jewels had all been taken from him. He possessed nothing but his suits of clothes and the few jewels he wore. The box contained some broken Garter Stars and two ornaments of St. George set with diamonds. His rings, and the magnificent Garter ornament were all he could bequeath to them. As he opened the box and kissing each child divided the few ornaments between them, he signalled the Bishop to come in.

"We have said our farewells," he said quietly, "and I have given to them all I have left to give in this world, except my blessing. Kneel down, my little ones."

He stood with his hand upon their heads, and asked God to protect and succor them in their orphancy, and as their father, he blessed them and asked that they pray for him.

Princess Elizabeth who was to die in her old prison at Carisbrooke Castle within a year, and the Prince who would not survive into his manhood, answered him together.

'Amen, Papa.'

"And now good-bye, my little ones. By tomorrow it will all be over. Do not forget me." He turned away from them and called out in a shaking voice to Juxon, "Bishop, take my children away now, I beg of you…."

Juxon caught both their hands and let them out. They had a last sight of their father who turned round, putting his handkerchief back in his pocket, and waved to them. He was smiling.

Execution

Cromwell had made a thorough preparation of erecting the scaffold at St. James Park near White Hall Palace. Attached to the scaffold were staples and ropes with which to tie the King to the wooden chopping block if he resisted. The time for public execution was fixed at 11 o'clock in the morning of January 30, 1649. A large crowd and soldiers had gathered to witness the execution. But the execution was delayed by three hours as the official executioner refused to do the job. Hurriedly another one was found, who agreed to do the work, provided he was allowed to wear a hood to hide his identity and given £100, then a huge amount. Though it was freezing cold, Charles appeared in black trousers and only a white silk shirt with cream cravat. He climbed the scaffold with unmatched dignity unaided by his captors. He kneeled on a white cushion and placed his neck on the chopping block. At that time, he was supposed to have told the executioner that he wished the chopping block was made higher for his comfort and said, 'Be quick.' Before executing the King, the executioner kneeled and said, 'Yes, Your Majesty.' And at 2 o'clock, the headman raised his axe and cut of his head with one blow. There was stunned silence for a few seconds. Some in the crowd surged forward with handkerchiefs to collect the spilt royal blood as souvenir while many sobbed and whispered 'Long live the King.' It is not known whether Cromwell was present on the occasion.

Charles' head was sewed to his body and he was taken to the White Hall Palace. After his relatives paid their last respects, the Crown King was laid to rest in the George Chappell of Windsor Castle.

Even today, visitors to the London Museum who come to see the crown jewels rarely fail to visit the scaffold and the headman's axe that had executed King Charles of England.

(f) Execution by Garotte[10]

In medieval times, if torture was intended, Garotte was employed where the victim would be made to stand or sit and a mechanical device such as a rack or a gag would be tightened around the person's neck, by turning the handle fixed in the back, causing slow strangulation, stretching and obstruction of blood vessels. A device could also be placed in a prisoner's mouth and kept in place by tying and locking a chain around his or her neck.

The other method of Garotte was a person being drowned and quartered while still alive before being garotted. For extremely serious crimes, such as high treason, hanging alone was not considered enough. Garotte was also a popular method of torture, and was similar to hanging.

□

3

Present Methods of Execution of Death Punishment

(a) Firing Squad[1]

Fig.[2]

There is no fixed procedure when it comes to execution by shooting. Nowadays, it is usually done inside the prison except during the contingency of war when a soldier is shot in the battlefield.

The traditional form of shooting can be carried out by a single executioner who fires from short range at the back of the head or neck as in China. The usual firing squad is made up of three to six shooters per prisoner who stand or kneel opposite the condemned person who is usually tied to a chair or to a stake. Normally, the shooters aim at the chest, since this is easier to hit than the head, causing rupture of the heart, great vessels, and lungs so that the condemned person dies of hemorrhage and shock. It is not unusual for the officer-in-charge to have to give the prisoner a pistol shot to the head to finish him off after the initial volley has failed to kill him.

In some countries, some rifles are loaded with blank bullets and the shooters are not told about it so that the true killer is unknown. Several countries like Russia and Eastern countries like Thailand use this method. It is significant to note that shooting by firing squad is also permitted in India when a death sentence is given by Court Martial.

The Utah statute authorising execution by firing squad only provides: "If the judgement of death is to be carried out by shooting, the executive director of the department or his designee shall select a five-person firing squad of officers." At the appropriate time, the condemned offender is led to the execution area or chamber, which is used for executions by both lethal injection and firing squad. The offender is placed in a specially designed chair, which has a pan beneath it to catch and conceal blood and other fluids. Restraints are applied to the offender's arms, legs, chest and head. A head restraint is applied loosely around the offender's neck to hold his neck and head in an upright position. The offender is dressed in a dark blue outfit with a white cloth circle attached by velcrum to the area over the offender's heart. Behind the offender are sandbags to absorb the volley. Approximately 20 feet directly in front of the offender is a wall. The weapons used are 30-30 caliber rifles. No special ammunition is used. Following the offender's statement, a hood is placed over his head. The warden leaves the room. The firing squad members stand in the firing position. They support their rifles on the platform rests. With their rifle barrels in the firing ports, the team members sight through open sights on the white cloth circle on the offender's chest. On the command to fire, the squad fires simultaneously. One squad member has a blank charge in his weapon but no member knows which member is designated to receive this blank charge (see Utah Execution Procedures).

In some states the United States like Utah and Oklahoma, choice is given to the convict, whether he should get the capital punishment by firing squad or by lethal injection. Gary Gilmore in 1977 and John Taylor in 1996 were executed by firing squad in Utah.

(b) Hanging by Noose[3]

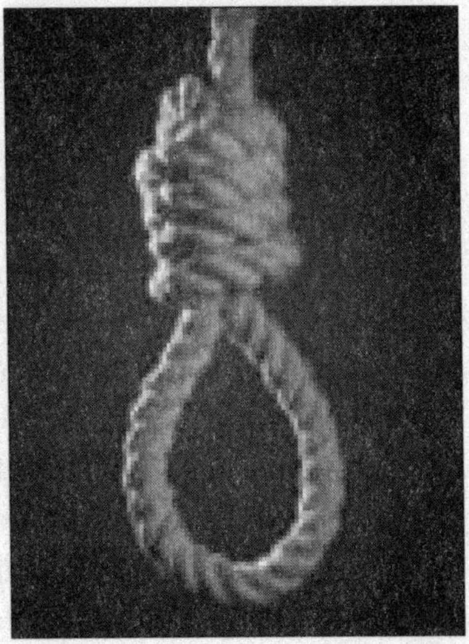

Hanging is a very common and old method adopted for execution among the various methods presently used. The prisoner could simply be hanged with a noose, which could lead to death by strangulation. However, the method of hanging known as 'long drop' is used to bring instantaneous death. This method of execution is today used in some countries including India and the States of Delaware, New Hampshire and Washington in the United States. But in the US hanging as a form of execution is used as an alternative to lethal injection, and the choice of this method is given to the prisoner.

In case of the use of hanging, the prisoner must be weighed prior to the execution. The 'drop' must be based on the prisoner's weight to deliver 1260 foot-pounds of force to the neck. The prisoner's weight in pounds is divided into 1260 to arrive at the drop in feet. The noose is then placed around the convict's neck, behind his or her left ear, which will cause the neck to snap. The trap door then opens and the convict drops. If properly done, death is caused by dislocation of the third and fourth cervical vertebrae. This lengthy measuring process is to assure almost instant death and a minimum of bruising. If careful measuring and planning is not done, strangulation, obstructed blood flow or beheading often result. Death by hanging, however, according to most of medico-jurisprudential writers, is the result of asphyxia or strangulation and fracture of the neck is an exception both in judicial and suicidal hanging. Jail manuals in India give a detailed procedure for judicial hanging which is given subsequently in Chapter 8.

Procedure in America[4]

Prior to any execution, the gallows area trap door and release mechanisms are inspected for proper operation. The rope, which is of manila hemp of at least 3/4" and not more than 1-1/4" in diameter and approximately 30 feet in length, is soaked and then stretched while drying to eliminate any spiraling, stiffness or tendency to coil. The hangman's knot, which is tied pursuant to military regulations, is treated with wax, soap or oil, to ensure that the rope slides smoothly through the knot. The end of the rope which does not contain the noose is tied to a grommet in the ceiling and is then tied to a metal T-shaped bracket, which takes the force delivered by the offender's drop.

Additionally, prior to an execution, the condemned offender's file is reviewed to determine if there are any unusual characteristics the offender possesses that might warrant deviation from field instructions on hanging. A physical examination and measuring process is conducted to assure almost instant death and a minimum of bruising. If careful measuring and planning is not done, strangulation, obstructed blood flow, or beheading could result. At the appropriate time on execution day, the inmate, in restrains, is escorted to the gallows area and is placed standing over a hinged trap door from which the offender will be dropped. Following the offender's last statement, a hood is placed over his head. Restrains are also applied. If the offender refuses to stand or cannot stand, he is placed on a collapse board. A determination of the proper amount of the drop of the condemned offender through the trap door is calculated using a standard military execution chart for hanging. The 'drop' must be based on the prisoner's weight, to deliver 1260 foot-pounds of force to the neck. The noose is then placed snugly around the convict's neck, behind his or her left ear, which will cause the neck to snap. The trap door then opens and the convict drops. If properly done, death is caused by dislocation of the third and fourth cervical vertebrae or by asphyxiation. A button mechanically releases the trap door and escorts then moves to the lower floor location to assist in the removal of the offender's body (see Washington Execution Procedures).

But there have been many cases of strangulation resulting in lingering torturous death and even decapitation if the length of the drop is short as found by post-mortem in the US and UK. This method of execution has, therefore, been given up in many States in the US. In India, which uses this method, there is no provision of post-mortem to find out whether a person died by breaking of the spinal cord or strangulation.

It is significant to note that leaders of the third Reich of Germany, who were given death punishment by hanging after the Nuremberg trials, asked for execution of death punishment by firing squad as the former was degrading and they wanted a military death. This reflects that death by hanging is not a dignified method of execution. Shooting of condemned prisoners is also followed under the military law in India in special cases.

(i) An Eye-Witness Account of Hanging – by George Orwell in 1931[5]

"I watched a man die once [in Burma]. There was no question that everyone concerned knew this to be dreadful, unnatural action. I believe it is always the same — the whole jail, wardens and prisoners alike are upset when there is an execution. It is probably they feel that capital punishment is accepted as necessary, and yet instinctively felt to be a wrong one, that gives so many descriptions of execution there a tragic atmosphere."

It was in Burma, a sodden morning of the rains. A sickly light, like yellow tinfoil, was slanting over the high walls into the jail yard. We were waiting outside the condemned cells, a row of sheds fronted with double bars, like small animal cages. Each cell measured about ten feet by ten and was quite bare within except for a plank bed and a pot of drinking water. In some of them, brown silent men were squatting at the inner bars, with their blankets draped round them. These were the condemned men, due to be hanged within the next week or two.

One prisoner had been brought out of his cell. He was a Hindu, a puny wisp of a man, with a shaven head and vague liquid eyes. He had a thick, sprouting moustache, absurdly too big for his body, rather like the moustache of a comic man on the films. Six tall Indian warders were guarding him and getting him ready for the gallows. Two of them stood by with rifles and fixed bayonets, while the others handcuffed him, passed a chain through his handcuffs and fixed it to their belts, and lashed his arms tight to his sides. They crowded very close about him, with their hands always on him in a careful, caressing grip, as though all the while feeling him to make sure he was there. It was like men handling a fish which is still alive and may jump back into the water. But he stood quite unresisting, yielding his arms limply to the ropes, as though he hardly noticed what was happening.

Eight o'clock struck and a bugle call, desolately thin in the wet air, floated from the distant barracks. The superintendent of the jail, who was standing apart from the rest of us, moodily prodding the gravel with his stick, raised his head at the sound. He was an army doctor, with a grey toothbrush moustache and a gruff voice. "For God's sake hurry up, Francis," he said irritably. "The man ought to have been dead by this time. Aren't you ready yet?"

Francis, the head jailer, a fat Dravidian in a white drill suit and gold spectacles, waved his black hand. 'Yes sir, yes sir,' he bubbled. "All is satisfactorily prepared. The hangman is waiting. We shall proceed."

"Well, quick march, then. The prisoners can't get their breakfast till this job's over."

We set out for the gallows. Two warders marched on either side of the prisoner, with their rifles at the slope; two others marched close against him, gripping him by arm and shoulder, as though at once pushing and supporting him. The rest of us, magistrates and the like, followed behind. Suddenly, when we had gone ten yards, the procession stopped short without any order or warning. A dreadful thing had happened–a dog, come goodness knows whence, had appeared in the yard. It came bounding among us with a loud volley of barks, and leapt round us wagging its whole body, wild with glee at finding so many human beings together. It was a large woolly dog, half Airedale, half pariah. For a moment, it pranced round us, and then, before anyone could stop it, it had made a dash for the prisoner, and jumping up tried to lick his face. Everyone stood aghast, too taken aback even to grab at the dog.

"Who let that bloody brute in here?" said the superintendent angrily. "Catch it, someone!"

A warder, detached from the escort, charged clumsily after the dog, but it danced and gambolled just out of his reach, taking everything as part of the game. A young Eurasian jailer picked up a handful of gravel and tried to stone the dog away, but it dodged the stones and came after us again. Its yaps echoed from the jail walls. The prisoner, in the grasp of the two warders, looked on incuriously, as though this was another formality of hanging. It was several minutes before someone managed to catch the dog. Then I put my handkerchief through its collar and moved off once more, with the dog still straining and whimpering.

It was about forty yards to the gallows. I watched the bare brown back of the prisoner marching in front of me. He walked clumsily with his bound arms, but quite steadily, with that bobbing gait of the Indian who never straightens his knees. At each step, his muscles slid neatly into place, the lock of hair on his scalp danced up and down, his feet printed themselves on the wet gravel. And once, inspite of the men who gripped him by each shoulder, he stepped slightly aside to avoid a puddle on the path.

It is curious, but till that moment I had never realised what it means to destroy a healthy, conscious man. When I saw the prisoner step aside to avoid the puddle, I saw the mystery, the unspeakable wrongness, of cutting a life short when it is in full tide. This man was not dying, he was alive just as we were alive. All the organs of his body were working — bowels digesting food, skin renewing itself, nails growing, tissues forming — all toiling away in solemn foolery. His nails would still be growing when he stood on the drop, when he was falling through the air with a tenth of a second to live. His eyes saw the yellow gravel and the grey walls, and his brain still remembered, foresaw, reasoned — reasoned even about puddles. He and we were a party of men walking together, seeing, hearing, feeling, understanding the same world; and in two minutes, with a sudden snap, one of us would be gone — one mind less, one world less.

The gallows stood in a small yard, separate from the main grounds of the prison, and overgrown with tall prickly weeds. It was a brick erection like three sides of a shed, with planking on top, and above that two beams and a crossbar with the rope dangling. The hangman, a grey-haired convict in the white uniform of the prison, was waiting beside his machine. He greeted us with a servile crouch as we entered. At a word from Francis the two warders, gripping the prisoner more closely than ever, half led, half pushed him to the gallows and helped him clumsily up the ladder. Then the hangman climbed up and fixed the rope round the prisoner's neck.

We stood waiting, five yards away. The warders had formed in a rough circle round the gallows. And then, when the noose was fixed, the prisoner began crying out on his God. It was a high, reiterated cry of 'Ram! Ram! Ram! Ram!', not urgent and fearful like a prayer or a cry for help, but steady, rhythmical, almost like the tolling of a bell. The dog answered the sound with a whine. The hangman, still standing on the gallows, produced a small cotton bag like a flour bag and drew it down over the prisoner's face. But the sound, muffled by the cloth, still persisted, over and over again: 'Ram! Ram! Ram! Ram! Ram!'

The hangman climbed down and stood ready, holding the lever. Minutes seemed to pass. The steady, muffled crying from the prisoner went on and on, 'Ram! Ram! Ram!' never faltering for an instant. The superintendent, his head on his chest, was slowly poking the ground with his stick; perhaps he was counting the cries, allowing the prisoner a fixed number — fifty, perhaps, or a hundred. Everyone had changed colour. The Indians had gone grey like bad coffee, and one or two of the bayonets were wavering. We looked at the hooded man on the drop, and listened to his cries — each cry another second of life; the same thought was in all our minds: oh, kill him quickly, get it over, stop that abominable noise!

Suddenly, the superintendent made up his mind. Throwing up his head, he made a swift motion with his stick. 'Chalo!' he shouted almost fiercely.

There was a clanking noise, and then dead silence. The prisoner had vanished, and the rope was twisting on itself. I let go of the dog, and it galloped immediately to the back of the gallows; but when it got there, it stopped short, barked and then retreated into a corner of the yard, where it stood among the weeds, looking remorously out at us. We went round the gallows to inspect the prisoner's body. He was dangling with his toes pointed straight downwards, very slowly revolving, as dead as a stone.

The superintendent reached out with his stick and poked the bare body; it oscillated, slightly. "He's all right," said the superintendent. He backed out from under the gallows, and blew out a deep breath. The moody look had gone out of his face quite suddenly. He glanced at his wrist-watch. "Eight minutes past eight. Well, that's all for this morning, thank God."

The warders unfixed bayonets and marched away. The dog, sobered and conscious of having misbehaved itself, slipped after them. We walked out of the gallows yard, past the condemned cells with their waiting prisoners, into the big central yard of the prison. The convicts, under the command of warders armed with lathis, were already receiving their breakfast. They squatted in long rows, each man holding a tin pannikin, while two warders with buckets marched round ladling out rice; it seemed quite a homely, jolly scene, after the hanging. An enormous relief had come upon us now that the job was done. One felt an impulse to sing, to break into a run, to snigger. All at once, everyone began chattering gaily.

The Eurasian boy walking beside me nodded towards the way we had come, with a knowing smile: "Do you know, sir, our friend (he meant the dead man), when he heard his appeal had been dismissed, he pissed on the floor of his cell. From fright. Kindly take one of my cigarettes, sir. Do you not admire my new silver case, sir? From the boxwallah, two rupees eight annas. Classy European style."

Several people laughed — at what, nobody seemed certain.

Francis was walking by the superintendent, talking garrulously. "Well, sir, all has passed off with the utmost satisfactoriness. It was all finished — flick! like that. It is not always so — oah, no! I have known cases where the doctor was obliged to go beneath the gallows and pull the prisoner's legs to ensure decease. Most disagreeable!"

"Wriggling about, eh? That's bad," said the superintendent.

"Ach, sir, it is worse when they become refractory! One man, I recall, clung to the bars of his cage when we went to take him out. You will scarcely credit, sir, that it took six warders to dislodge him, three pulling at each leg. We reasoned with him. 'My dear fellow,' we said, 'think of all the pain and trouble you are causing to us!' But no, he would not listen! Ach, he was very troublesome!"

I found that I was laughing quite loudly. Everyone was laughing. Even the superintendent grinned in a tolerant way. "You'd better all come out and have a drink," he said quite genially. "I've got a bottle of whisky in the car. We could do with it."

We went through the big double gates of the prison, into the road. "Pulling at his legs!" exclaimed a Burmese magistrate suddenly, and burst into a loud chuckling. We all began laughing again. At that moment, Francis's anecdote seemed extraordinarily funny. We all had a drink together, native and European alike, quite amicably. The dead man was a hundred yards away.

(ii) Controversial Hanging of Timothy John Evans in 1950[6]

Wrong Execution which raised unprecedented controversy and resulted in abolition of death penalty in Britain

Timothy Evans (Centre), being escorted by police, was hanged on March 9, 1950 for killing his daughter Geraldine[7]

Timothy John Evans was arrested and accused of murdering his wife and daughter at their residence in London in November 1949. In January 1950, Evans was tried and convicted of the murder of his daughter and sentenced to death by hanging. During his trial, Evans had accused his neighbour, John Christie, of being responsible for the murders. Evans was put on trial for the murder of his 13-month-old daughter, Geraldine, and his wife on January 11, 1950. He had recanted his confession and alleged that Christie had always been responsible for the murders. This was the basis of Evans' defence in his trial, which he maintained as the truth until his execution. Subsequent events were to confirm the veracity of Evans' beliefs. He was a truck driver with no previous criminal history.

Christie and his wife, Ethel, were key witnesses for the prosecution. Christie gave detailed evidence about the quarrels between Evans and his wife. The defence sought to show how Christie was the murderer by highlighting his past criminal record. Christie had previous convictions for several thefts and malicious wounding. The latter case involved Christie striking a woman on the head with a cricket bat. But his apparent reformation, and his service with the police, impressed the jury. The defence also could not find a motive for why a supposedly respectable person like Christie would want to murder two people, whereas the prosecution could use the explanation in Evans' confessions as his motive for wanting to kill the victims. Evans had no criminal record. Had the police conducted a thorough search of the garden and found the bones of two prior victims of Christie, the trial may not have occurred at all, and a serial killer prevented from murdering again. However, Evans' reputation for conflicting statements fatally undermined his credibility. That reputation was created by the police themselves in preparing several false confessions, forcing Evans to incriminate himself with threats of violence. The case largely came down to Christie's word against Evans' and the course of the trial rapidly turned against Evans. The trial itself lasted only three days and much key evidence was omitted, or never shown to the jury. The judge was prejudiced against Evans from the start, and his summing up was biased against the defendant. Evans was found guilty two days later — the jury taking just 40 minutes to come to its decision. After his appeal to the House of Lords was dismissed, he was hanged on March 9, 1950.

This outcome was severely criticised when Christie's murders were discovered three years later. During interviews with the police and psychiatrists prior to his execution, Christie admitted several times that he had been responsible for the murder of Beryl Evans. If these confessions were true, Evans' second statement detailing Christie's offer to abort Beryl's baby is the true version of events that took place at Rillington Place. One Ludovic Kennedy provided one possible reconstruction of how the murder took place, where an unsuspecting Beryl lets Christie into her apartment, expecting the abortion to be carried out, but is instead attacked and then strangled. Christie claimed to have possibly engaged in sexual intercourse with Beryl's body after her death.

One important fact was not brought up in Evans' trial: several workmen were willing to testify that there were no bodies in the wash-house when they worked there several days after Evans supposedly hid them. They stored their tools in the wash-room, and mended the roof during this period. Their evidence in itself would have raised doubts about the veracity of Evans' alleged confessions, but the workmen were not called to give evidence. Indeed, the police re-interviewed the workmen and forced them to change their evidence to fit the preconceived idea that Evans was the sole murderer. The murderer, Christie, would have hidden the bodies of Beryl and Geraldine in the temporarily vacant first-floor flat, and then moved them to the wash-house four days later when the workmen had finished. Christie had used a similar procedure in both his previous murders of Fuerst and Eady according to his confession in 1953.

The public was very exercised over the wrongful execution of Evans. As a result of a prolonged campaign, the Home Secretary, Sir Frank Soskice, ordered an inquiry chaired by High Court Judge Sir Daniel Brabin in 1965-66. Brabin found it was "more probable than not" that Evans murdered his wife and that he did not murder his daughter. This was contrary to the prosecution case in Evans' trial, which held that both murders had been committed by the same person as a single transaction. The victims' bodies had been found together in the same location and had been murdered in the same way by strangulation. Despite his conclusion, the Brabin enquiry exposed police malpractice during the Evans case such as destruction of evidence. The neck tie which had been used to strangle Geraldine, for example, was destroyed by the police prior to the discovery of Christie's crimes in 1953. Even the record book, in which the destruction had to be noted, was itself destroyed by the police. In most serious cases, police are required to preserve all material and documentary evidence, so the removal of evidence in this case was suspicious. Many police statements were contradictory and confused as to dates and times of interviews with key witnesses, especially of the Christies during the first murder case. Brabin went to great lengths to prefer police evidence wherever possible, and exonerate them of any police misconduct. This enquiry did little to settle the many issues which arose from the case.

Therefore, Soskice's successor as Home Secretary recommended a royal pardon for Evans, which was granted in October 1966. The outcry over the Evans' case contributed to raising the question of wrongful execution in the British Parliament. A number of Members of Parliament, like Michal Foot, raised their voice against death penalty with the result that it was abolished in 1966.

Not only that, in January 2003 the Home Office awarded Timothy Evans's half-sister, Mary Westlake, and his sister, Eileen Ashby, *ex-gratia* payments as compensation for the miscarriage of justice in Evans's trial. The independent assessor for the Home Office, Lord Brennan QC, accepted that "the conviction and execution of Timothy Evans for the murder of his child was wrongful and a miscarriage of justice" and that "there is no evidence to implicate Timothy Evans in the murder of his wife. She was most probably murdered by Christie." Lord Brennan believed that the Brabin report's conclusion that Evans probably murdered his wife should be rejected given Christie's confessions and conviction.

On November 16, 2004, Evans's sister Mary began an appeal in the High Court to overturn a decision by the Criminal Cases Review Commission not to refer the Evans case to the Court of Appeal to have his conviction formally quashed. She argued that Evans' pardon had not formally expunged his conviction of murdering his daughter, and although the Brabin report had concluded that Evans probably did not kill his daughter, it had not declared him innocent. The report also contained the 'devastating' conclusion that Evans had probably killed his wife. The request to refer the case was dismissed on November 19, 2004, with the judges saying that the cost and resources of quashing the conviction could not be justified, although they did accept that Evans did not murder either his wife or his child.

The case ranks as one of the most serious miscarriages of justice in the post-war period caused by a combination of police incompetence and willful selection of the facts to ensnare a completely innocent man.

Although there have been cases of innocent persons being executed in the USA and elsewhere, no country other than the

UK has ever held an enquiry or posthumously pardon the victim and paid damages.

(c) Electrocution[8]

Before electrocution, hanging, though gruesome, was the number one method of carrying out capital punishment. A New York dentist, Albert Southwick, saw an old drunken man accidentally getting electrocuted by falling on an electric generator with no pain or wound on his body. He told a friend in the legislature and the idea of executing people using the modern marvel of electricity began to take hold.

Beginning in 1886, the New York State Government established a legislative commission to study the alternate forms of capital punishment. Southwick soon became a part of the commission in charge of studying the feasibility or replacing hanging with electrocution.

Two electrical companies, viz. General Electric Company (founded by Thomas Edison) and Westinghouse Corporation invented the electric chair, the former using the DC service and the latter the AC service.

However, since two potential designs (AC and DC) of the electric chair existed, it was left to a government committee to decide which form to choose. Doctor Peterson was the head of the government committee to select the best design for an electric chair, and the committee opted for the AC design. The first electric chair designed for an execution was created by Westinghouse at the turn of the century. Westinghouse stated before the committee that the electric chair's power source was so deadly that it would take only five seconds of 1,000 volts to cause death. On June 4, 1888, Section 505 of Chapter 488 of Criminal Procedure Code of New York was amended to read as under:

> "The punishment of death must, in every case, be inflicted by causing to pass through the body of the convict a current of electricity of sufficient intensity to cause death, and the application of such current must be continued until such convict is dead."

New York State was the first one to use this method. Since then, this form of carrying out execution captured American popular imagination for around a hundred years.

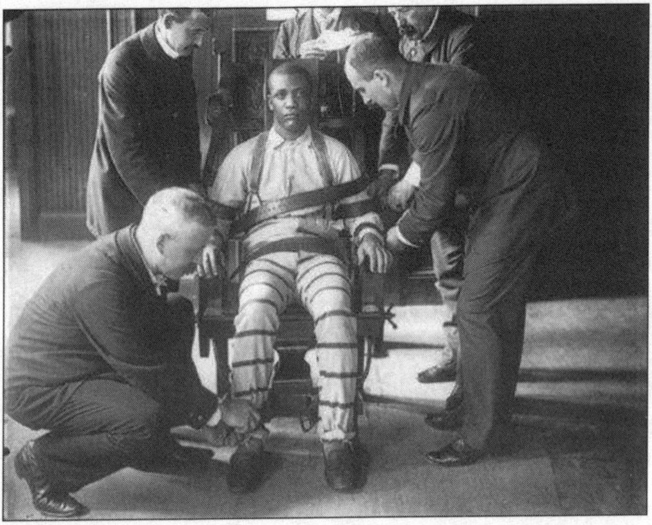

William Kemmler, an African American prisoner, was the first man to be executed by electrocution in 1890. (Image courtesy Library of Congress)[9]

However, this method is now on the way out because of the pain and gruesome injury it causes to the victim besides the mutilation of body. The first man to be executed by an electric chain, William Kemmler, did not die in five seconds but was finally pronounced dead after four minutes of steady stream of power going through his body. During those four minutes, the body of the convict started to smoke, the hair on his arms and head went up in flames, and blood spilled from every orifice on his face. After this display, the electric chair was considered a failure. Today the electric chair has been modernised but it still causes agonising death.

In a typical execution using the electric chair, a prisoner is strapped to a specially built chair, his head and body shaved to provide better contact with moistened copper electrodes that the executioner attaches. Usually, three or more executioners push buttons, but only one is connected to the actual electrical source and, therefore, the real executioner is not known. The jolt varies in power from state to state, and is also determined by the convict's body weight. The first jolt is followed by several more in a lower voltage. In Georgia, executioners apply 2,000 volts for four seconds, 1,000 volts for the next seven seconds and then 208 volts for two minutes. Electrocution produces visibly destructive effects on the body, as the internal organs are burned. The prisoner usually leaps forward against the restrains when the switch is turned on. The body changes colour, swells and may even catch fire. The prisoner may also defecate, urinate and vomit blood.

The execution protocol for most states authorises the use of a wooden chair with restraints and connections to an electric current. The offender enters the execution chamber and is placed in the electric chair. The chair is constructed of oak and is set on rubber matting and bolted to a concrete floor. Lap, chest, arm and forearm straps are secured. A leg piece (anklet) is laced to the offender's right calf and a sponge and electrode is attached. The headgear consists of a metal headpiece covered with a leather hood which conceals the offender's face. The metal part of the headpiece consists of a copper wire mesh screen to which the electrode is brazened. A wet sponge is placed between the electrode and the offender's scalp. The circuit breaker is engaged and the execution control panel is activated. The automatic cycle begins with the programmed 2,300 volts for eight seconds, followed by 1,000 volts (4 AMPs) for 22 seconds, followed by 2,300 volts (9.5 AMPs) for eight seconds. When the cycle is complete, the equipment is disconnected and the manual circuit behind the chair is disengaged. If the offender is not pronounced dead, the execution cycle is then repeated (see Florida Execution Procedures).

The most common problems encountered include burning of varying degrees to parts of the body, and a failure of the procedures to cause death without repeated shocks. Witness accounts of many botched executions over the years have caused electrocution to be replaced with lethal injection as the most common method of execution.

Today, electrocution is used in eleven States of USA. But Arkansas, Kentucky, Ohio, Oklahoma, South Carolina, Tennessee and Virginia authorise both lethal injection and electrocution, allowing the inmates to choose one of these methods. Till 2004, electrocution had been declared unconstitutional in Alabama, Florida, Georgia and Nebraska. Since 1976, 144 people have been executed by electric chair.

Controversial Execution of Rosenbergs in 1953[10]

The execution of the Rosenberg couple, Michel and Ethel, was by far the most controversial. It evoked demonstrations on both sides of the Atlantic and even after half a century their trial, judgement and punishment continues to be a subject of debate. The tense atmosphere of the Cold War, casualties suffered by the Americans during the Korean War, the outburst of Secretary of State Allan Dulles, "If you are not with us, you are against us," which described the non-aligned nations, have all contributed to create a hysterical atmosphere in the United States.

Judge Iriving Kaus, by his judgement dated April 5, 1951, found the Rosenbergs guilty and sentenced them to death for passing atomic secrets to the Soviet Union during World War II, which helped the Soviets to break the atomic monopoly of the Americans. He also found them responsible for the tens of thousands of deaths in the Korean War.

Michael and Ethel Rosenberg[11]

The death punishment was followed by appeals, writ petitions, stays and final rejection of clemency plea by President Dwight Eisenhower. It was a solitary case in the American history of execution of one of its citizen for treason. The judgement was based on evidence of accomplices and persons found guilty of the same charges like Klaus Fulton and Martian Sable who were given imprisonment. Eminent Nobel Laureates like Albert Einstein in the US, Hubel Urge in Europe and even Pope Pious XI had appealed to the President of the US to spare their lives. Demonstrations with bill-boards demanding 'Save Rosenberg' and 'Kill Rosenberg' continued in America and all over Europe till the end.

This is the story of the last days of Rosenbergs before the electric chair extinguished their lives on June 19, 1953.

On Friday, June 19, 1953, Ethel and Julius were informed by Warden/Jailor Denno that the Supreme Court had vacated the stay. Execution was scheduled that night at 11 p.m.

They knew that there were frantic efforts to have President Dwight Eisenhower save them. Anticipating the worst, they wrote a final letter to their children, Michael, 9 and Robert, 5. In a covering letter, Ethel requested their attorney Manny Bloch to deliver it to their children. This letter reads:

"Dearest Sweethearts, my most precious children:

Only this morning it looked like we might be together again after all. Now that this cannot be, I want so much for you to know all that I have come to know. Unfortunately, I may write only a few simple words; the rest your own lives must teach you, even as mine taught me.

At first, of course, you will grieve bitterly for us, but you will not grieve alone. That is our consolation and it must eventually be yours.

Eventually, too, you must come to believe that life is worth the living. Be comforted that even now, with the end of ours slowly approaching, we know this with a conviction that defeats the executioner!

Your lives must teach you, too, that good cannot really flourish in the midst of evil; that freedom and all the things that go to make up a truly satisfying and worthwhile life must sometimes be purchased very dearly. Be comforted, then, that we were serene and understood with the deepest kind of understanding that civilisation had not as yet progressed to the point where life did not have to be lost for the sake of life; and that we were comforted in the sure knowledge that others would carry on after us.

We wish we might have had the tremendous joy and gratification of living our lives out with you. Your Daddy, who is with me in these last momentous hours, sends his heart and all the love that is in it for his dearest boys. Always remember that we were innocent and could not wrong our conscience.

We press you close and kiss you with all our strength.

Lovingly, Daddy and Mommy

Julie, Ethel

P.S. to Manny — The Ten Commandments religious medal and cham — and my wedding ring — I wish you to present to our children as a token of our undying love."

Emanuel H. Bloch, defence attorney, accompanying Rosenberg children Michael, 10, and Robert, 6, on June 16, 1953 after seeing their parents for the last time in the Sing Sing Prison[12]

In the meantime, Bloch had the idea that a delay of execution might be obtained on religious grounds and he phoned Solicitor General Robert Stern that the Sabbath began at sunset on Friday and ended Saturday at sunset. He pleaded that it was only one day he was asking. Stern undertook to submit the matter immediately to the Attorney General, "Please do it quickly," urged Bloch, "You know as there was little time." Just then a reporter dashed in his house stating that President Eisenhower had issued a statement in the afternoon of January 18, 1953 refusing to grant clemency. It read:

> "When in their most solemn judgement the tribunals of the States have adjudged them guilty and their sentence just and can't intervene in this matter. The execution of two human beings is a grave matter; graver is the thought of the millions of dead whose death, directly attributable to what these spies have done…"

Fig.[13]

Bloch and members of the Rosenberg family hurried to the White House for a personal meeting with the President with Ethel's letter hoping it will move the President. The meeting was denied but the White House official informed them that the letter had been delivered to the President himself.

Shortly thereafter, another announcement came from the White House. "The President has read the letter of the defendant Ethel Rosenberg. He states that in his conviction it adds nothing to the issues covered in his statement of this afternoon."

The President had also declined to see Sophie Rosenberg, sister of Julius.

There was a pause in the avalance of bad news. A radio flash announced that the Attorney General had ordered that the executions would not violate the Sabbath. "This will give us twenty-four more hours," Bloch said. "We must reach the President in person."

Fearful that there might be some failure of communication with Sing Sing prison, he asked that Warden Denno be called. The room was crowded with lawyers and reporters. He called for silence as he got on the phone.

"Warden Denno? This is Mr. Bloch. We're calling, Warden, just to confirm the fact that the executions are delayed until Saturday night you know — on account of the Sabbath."

There was a pause followed by Bloch's scream.

"What? Moved ahead? My God, eight o'clock! It is seven-thirty now, My God — no!"

Something snapped in him and he went berserk. He, however, phoned US Marshal William A. Carroll and said, "This is Manny Bloch. Please tell Julius and Ethel I did the best I could for them. Tell them I will take care of the children. Tell them I love them. Tell them..." and he broke down in uncontrollable sobs.

Earlier Bloch travelled for two years from coast to coast, giving talks on the Rosenberg case and raised $45,000 for the education and maintenance of Michael and Robert. He succeeded and every cent was used meticulously for the purpose for which it was raised.

Besides, the Rosenberg Committee had collected and spent approximately one million dollars. Indeed, the Treasury Department filed a lien for $124,900 in unpaid taxes against the committee (which had failed to qualify for tax exemption).

There were jeers but also prayers by millions of people for the Rosenberg children and their parents. Two thousand families in the US and Europe offered to adopt them. So strong was the reaction that State Department of the United States sent a review of the case to forty of its diplomatic missions throughout the world, outlining the charges, the evidence and the numerous appeals to clear misunderstandings that the case involved free speech or that there was no evidence of guilt. Protests throughout the world reached an ugly climax as the execution hour drew near. Hourly bulletins were broadcast of the state of affairs which still were uncertain. Would a last-second stay come from somewhere somehow? Even if such a miracle did not occur, there was the possibility that the Rosenbergs would crack under pressure and confess and thereby earn a commutation of the death sentence. These uncertainties persisted until the very moment the switch was to be pulled. Never before had the law's final act hovered in suspense so long.

Fearing demonstrations outside the prison walls, the state and Federal Government had taken special precautions. State troopers and police barricaded all approaches to Sing Sing prison. They were trained and prepared to prevent any public demonstration.

As if the turbulence outside and abroad had communicated itself to the two thousand inmates of the prison, there was unusual tension and unrest within its walls. This had nothing to do with any view of the guilt or innocence of the Rosenbergs. Execution night always brought out a collective prison instinct among the inmates of abhorrence when death is to be inflicted. There was rattling of cups, banging the iron gates, whistling and cursing, in revolt against their enslavement. Their feelings were heightened by the fact that 'stool pigeons' had convicted the Rosenbergs, and even worse, one of them [Greenglass] had sent his own sister to the chair. They resented the breach of their own criminal code.

It was a sweltering day. Thirty-five perspiring newspapermen and women were in the downstairs waiting room of the prison. Every few seconds their eyes turned to the clock on the wall as if its message had to be continuously confirmed.

In the execution chamber, this being a federal rather than a state execution, only five witnesses were permitted. They were US Marshal William Carroll, his deputy, Thomas Farley, and three representatives of the major news services: Bob Considine of International News Service and the Hearst newspapers, Relmin Morin of the Associated Press and Jack Wolison of United Press.

In Washington, the Attorney General waited in his office for word either that the executions had taken place or that the Rosenbergs had accepted the government's offer to escape death, if they confessed and informed who their co-conspirators were. There was an open telephone line direct to Sing Sing prison in the event of last-minute repentance. The warden and US Marshal Carroll had advised the Rosenbergs that the offer conveyed to them by Federal Prison Director Bennett remained until the last moment, should they change their minds.

Marshal Carroll was in the death house together with three FBI men to stop the execution if either Julius or Ethel signalled repentance.

Electrocution of Michel

Their gruesome preparation for execution began in the morning. All of Julius' possessions were removed from his cell. His books, pictures of his sons, and his clothes and undergarments, all were taken, even shoelaces, belts, razor blades, a small looking glass or anything which might be utilised for suicide were removed. The illusion that he had built a little home was shattered. The cell and he were left stripped. He was given his last garments, fresh khaki pants, a loose T-shirt and buff-coloured slippers to put on naked feet.

Ethel received a cheap green dress with white polka dots and terry-cloth slippers — nothing else. The advancement of the death hour to eight o'clock made it the first 'daytime' execution in the prison's history. It allowed no time for the famous last meal. The Rosenbergs refused any sustenance and chose to spend the remaining time talking to each other. A mesh screen was set up in front of her cell and she was permitted to leave the cell and sit on a chair facing Julius on the other side of the screen. The matrons and guards were instructed to stand back far enough so that they could converse privately.

At 7.20 p.m., the guard moved up behind Julius and put his hand on his shoulder. He knew that he had to be prepared for his death at eight. He put two fingers to his lips and pressed them towards Ethel on the mesh screen. She did the same. They pressed so hard that the tips of their fingers bled as they touched through the mesh. This was their good-bye kiss.

A guard and prison barber were waiting for Julius in his cell. The back of his head was shaved to permit the electrode to make direct contact with his scalp.

The guard scissored a slit up one leg of his pants to the knee to make room for another electrode on his calf. The barber shaved that area. Then the guard sewed the slit together loosely, so that it wouldn't flap when he took his last walk.

Julius sat numb throughout it all, as if nature had mercifully rendered him unconscious of his surroundings. He was startled when at two minutes to eight the prison chaplain, Rabbi Irving Koslowe, thirty-five years old, appeared in black robe and yarmulke (skull cap) and said, "Julius, follow me."

Two guards entered and took him by the arms. They began the march down the narrow concrete corridor towards the death chamber.

The chaplain was reading the 23rd Psalm, "The Lord is my shepherd, I shall not want…" Julius, pale, thin and numb with terror, shuffled behind him, partly supported by the guards. His eyes were red, but dry. There were no tears left. He was breathing rapidly.

As he entered the death chamber, the glare of the lights, made stronger by the white walls, made him stop and blink in horror. The chair in the centre of the room, bolted to the concrete floor with metal braces, was made of oak wood, which acted as a non-conductor. It had wide wooden straps and wires dangled underneath.

His eyes were dimmed by fright. He saw none of the witnesses or others in the room. His ears were probably deaf to all but the pounding of his heart. His legs gave way. The guards held him up firmly, and dragged him towards the death chair. There they turned him and lowered him, like an invalid, into it. Another guard dipped his fingers in a jar, and with a circular motion, rubbed the adhesive paste on the shaven part of the head. Then he knelt and rubbed conductive paste on his calf.

Thereafter, he placed electrodes with attached wet sponges on both areas.

After a guard had removed Julius' eyeglasses, folded them gently and put them aside, they proceeded to strap him into the chair.

His hands were clenched in his lap. The guards forced them apart and strapped them at the wrists to the arms of the chair. His fingers seized the edge of the chair and turned white squeezing it, as if it was his support rather than the instrument of death. Another brown strap was tied across his lap, his chest and around his head. He was breathing fast and with effort. His eyes were closed tight. His lips were sucked in. Then a wide black leather hood was dropped over his head. This was not as much a merciful act for him as it was to protect witnesses and others from the sight of fractured lenses of the eyes, a blue burnt tongue, and fearful distortions of the muscles, as they were convulsed by shock.

The executioner was Joseph Francel, an electrician from Cairo, New York. He had performed this service for fourteen years and was paid $150 for each execution. He took his place behind a glass panel in an alcove. The warden stepped forward. It was precisely eight o'clock. He nodded. The electrician pulled a huge switch downward in a firm unhurried movement.

Two thousand volts, delivered at the maximum eight amperes, crashed Julius violently against the straps. For thirty seconds, the crackling noise of the current continued, as his body snapped back and forth like a whip, the straps creaking from the strain. His neck seemed to grow several sizes. Yellow-gray smoke rose in wisps from his head.

The current was turned off. The rigid straining body collapsed limply. As the whining noise stopped, a deadly silence pervaded the room. It was broken by a second charge, reduced to five hundred volts at four amperes to prevent 'cooking.' It continued for fifty-seven seconds.

Again, there were sizzling noises and an involuntary spastic dance of the body against the straps. When the switch was released, Julius' body collapsed like a puppet dropped unceremoniously. A third charge of less voltage was given to be certain that all bodily functions had been deranged and death insured. After fifty seconds, the switch was lifted; Julius was hanging limply over the straps.

The prison physician, Dr. George McCracken, standing with his young assistant, Dr. H.W. Kipp, directly to one side of the chair, stepped forward. He ripped the T-shirt, applied the stethoscope, nodded and said as required by law, "I pronounce this man dead!" He wiped his upper lip with the back of his hand.

There was a hideous stench in the room of burning flesh, urine and defecation. The guards stepped forward and untied the straps. They lifted Julius onto a gurney, which a third guard had brought into the room, and wheeled him out into the autopsy room.

A fourth guard entered with a mop and bucket. He wiped off the seat with a dark brown sponge. He mopped up the puddle underneath the chair and left a powerful scent of ammonia to disguise the smell of an involuntary death to prepare for the second electrocution.

Double Electrocution of Ethel

Rabbi Koslowe walked sadly out of the chamber to lead Ethel to her death. She was to be the eighth woman in Sing Sing's history to be electrocuted. When he arrived in her cell, she said, "Did it happen!"

"Yes, he is dead."

She sat still, showing no emotion.

"Ethel, for the sake of the children who need you, will you say something which can still save you? Must this tragedy be completed?"

She rose. "I have nothing to say. I am ready." Two gray-haired matrons offered their arms which she ignored. She walked past them and behind the chaplain with steady steps.

Rabbi Koslowe chanted from Psalm 31:

"For I have heard the slander of many;

Fear was on every side,…"

As she passed Julius' cell, she paused, looked into its emptiness, lowered her head and moved her lips silently perhaps in fleeting dedication to his memory. Then she lifted her head high and walked forward resolutely.

As she entered the white room, the skylight over the black chair had turned bluish purple from the night, the glare of the chamber light replacing it.

Unlike Julius, she was composed. Her controlled serenity created a heroic impression. She had a Mona Lisa smile, but with an edge of bitterness, and looked every witness in the eye. Some could not return her gaze.

She stopped in front of the chair and held out her hand to her matron, Mrs. Helen Evans, who had become her friend in the last two years. The matron took it hesitantly. Ethel drew her close and brushed her cheek with a tender kiss. The matron ran out of the room, dabbing her eyes. Then in another royal gesture, she shook the hand of the other matron.

She turned and placed herself in the chair, refusing any helping hand, and watched the guards strap her in as if it was an inconsequential act on an airplane. She herself shifted in the chair to help them place the leather bands across her. She tucked in her leg to help a guard adjust its strap.

However, when the electrode with the wet sponge touched her shaven scalp, she lost her beautific expression for a moment and winced. Then she cocked her head to help the placement of the monstrous black crown on her head.

The warden signalled with a nod. Francel walked quickly into the alcove. He pulled the switch down. Her body smashed convulsively against the straps which made creaking noises under the strain. Combined with the whistling, crackling sound of electricity, they created weird, rhythmic dissonances, as if witches were howling in the wind.

Her right index finger rose as if in silent rebuke. Her body lifted off the seat against the straps and her hands closed into fists as if she was going to charge across the room swinging.

There was a strong smell of burning flesh, as the temperature of her body reached 140 degrees. Thin smoke rose from her scalp and turned blue in the overhead light, as it flattened out in an ugly cake against the skylight overhead.

After the three long shocks, the switch was turned off.

The body hung loose. The silence and stench mixed. A guard unleashed the black strap that had been tied tightly across her breasts. Another guard unbound her arms and a leg. Dr. McCracken approached. He could not place his stethoscope through the collar of the dress. He and Dr. Kipp tore it open and listened to her heart. The doctor stepped back bewildered. Instead of uttering the ritual words, he looked at the warden and said in a hollow voice, "This woman is still alive."

The executioner came out from his alcove to consult with the warden and the doctor. They, too, could not believe that there was still a heartbeat. In a whispered conference, they decided to turn the switch on for a severe and then modified jolt.

The guards re-strapped her for a second execution. The warden signalled again. The switch was pulled down. For fifty-seven seconds, her body bounced in convulsive movements against the straps, while sizzling skillet noises crackled in the room. The switch was lifted. She descended into the seat in slow motion. Another jolt for fifty-seven seconds made sputtering noises and sent a plume of smoke out of her head. Then there was silence and collapse. The doctor applied his stethoscope to the smoldering chest. He straightened and said, "I pronounce this woman dead."

Two guards untied the straps, lifted her onto a wheel table. Her right leg was flexed in a nonchalant posture as they pushed her out to the autopsy room.

It had taken two minutes and forty-five seconds to kill Julius, and four minutes and thirty seconds to destroy Ethel. She died after sundown at 8.17 on the Sabbath.

On the evening of the execution, the kind woman with whom the children were staying sought to shield Michael from the shock. There was a baseball game between the New York Yankees and Detroit Tigers on television. She lured him into watching it. She had underestimated the overriding interest in the case. Suddenly, there was a fearful scream like those that ejected him from his nightmares. A bulletin had flashed across the screen: "President Eisenhower has turned down Ethel and Julius' final appeal. They must die tonight."

She rushed into the room and found Michael curled up in a corner of the big leather chair in a fetal position, whimpering. With difficulty, she lifted him in her arms and carried him to bed, where she held him tenderly during the sleepless night.

Fig.[14]

Rosenberg Case – Legal Murder That Haunts American Histroy[15]

The Rosenberg funeral was marred by political harangue and controversy as their lives. As many as thirty thousand people surrounded the I.J. Morris Funeral Home at Church Avenue in Brooklyn, New York, which could hold only 310 mourners. The family split in court persisted at the funeral. Julius' mother and two sisters attended but no one from the Greenglass family came to pay respect to Ethel and Michael in death.

Joseph Brainin, Chairman of the Rosenberg Committee, introduced the speakers. He described his committee as "representing a cross-section of America."

Three chartered buses and three hundred private automobiles followed the two hearses to Wellwood Cemetery at Pine Lawn, near Farmingdale, Long Island. There Ethel, thirty-seven, and Julius, thirty-five, were interred. Acrimony accompanied them to the grave.

Emanuel H. Bloch and Rabbi Abraham Cronbach, an elderly professor emeritus of the Hebrew Union College of Cincinnati, were among the speakers.

After the service, there was violence outside the chapel, despite the presence of more than two hundred foot patrolmen, mounted and motorcycle police and dozens of detectives.

What had been drowned out in the fury of the protest movement was the sober opinion of the American people. Editorials in leading newspapers throughout the land expressed the view that the Rosenbergs had their full and fair day in court by the unprecedented appellate procedures and they discounted much of the criticism as Communist inspired.

Typical of these was *The New York Times* editorial of March 30, 1951:

"They have denied their guilt and have appealed their case. But to the layman, it must seem that they have been convicted after a fair trial, and that their conviction rests on the testimony of their own self-confessed accomplices in a spy ring which centered around the convicted British scientist Klaus Fuchs, and was headed by a master spy disguised as a Soviet Vice Consul in New York…."

Justice William O. Douglous of the US Supreme Court granted stay of the execution on June 17, 1953. It was thought the stay would continue for some months as the Court was on vacation. But the Bench of the Supreme Court assembled the very next day and vacated the stay on the morning of June 19, 1953. Justice Douglous in his autobiography referring to the Rosenbergs gave a sense of poignant ambience in which they were tried and executed, when he wrote, "Many lives were blighted in the midst of the Cold War, and not a few shortened, but the Rosenbergs alone were directly 'legally' murdered by the State. The extent of transgression of 'due process of law and equal justice under law' that resulted in killing has been unequalled in century — in terms of murder by their politics…."

It is significant to note that in 1978, the very government which 25 years ago spent close to one million dollars in prosecuting the Rosenbergs, sanctioned the fund through the Corporation of Public Broadcasting for recrimination of the case.[17]

In 1989, Boris V. Brokhovich, the Soviet Director of Proscenium Production and Extraction Facility for the first Soviet Atomic Bomb, denied the Rosenbergs' involvement in leaking US atomic secrets. He said, "You sat Rosenberg in the electric chair for nothing. We got nothing from Rosenberg."

However, on the fiftieth anniversary of the Rosenbergs' execution, the same *The New York Times* in a telling long editorial on June 19, 2003, wrote:

> "Despite several appeals and a worldwide campaign for mercy, they were executed at Sing Sing Prison in 1953, the only US civilians ever executed for espionage, despite considerable controversy in subsequent years....
>
> The decision to execute the Rosenbergs was, and still is, controversial.... The Rosenbergs case still haunts American history, reminding us of the injustice that can be done when a nation gets caught up in hysteria. This hysteria had both an immediate and a lasting effect; many innocent scientists, including some who were virulently anti-communist, were investigated simply for having the last name 'Rosenberg'. The other atomic spies who were caught by the FBI offered confessions and were not executed. Ethel's brother, David Greenglass, who supplied documents to Julius from Los Alamos, served 10 years of his 15-year sentence. Harry Gold, who identified Greenglass, served 15 years in Federal prison as the courier for Greenglass and the British scientist, Klaus Fuchs. Morton Sobell, who was tried with the Rosenbergs, served

17 years and 9 months of a 30-year sentence. In 2008, Sobell admitted he was a spy and confirmed Julius Rosenberg was 'in a conspiracy that delivered to the Soviets classified military and industrial information and what the American government described as the secret to the atomic bomb'."

However, the death penalty was unfortunate from every viewpoint. The crime was serious enough to warrant it, but the disparity of punishment given to others who were equally guilty resulted in uneven justice, which is equivalent to injustice.

Also, there were humanistic considerations. Even a thirty-year sentence would have deprived the Rosenberg children of a father's and mother's care, but it was worse to orphan them. It increased the horror of execution.

There were other peripheral reasons to avoid the extreme penalty. The Rosenbergs were convicted chiefly on the testimony of accomplices. There is a long existing contention that allowance should be made for possible irresponsibility of such a source, so as to preclude death sentence in such a case.

Also, there was the heated atmosphere of the 1950s against communism, which led many to believe that the most careful instructions could not overcome its prejudice. All this argued for a merciful penalty, either at the hands of the judge or the President.

The terrible ordeal of the trial, the scenes in the death house with the children, and the final hours of torment had a telling effect on the health of the Rosenbergs' attorney. He died shortly afterwards.

Alexander Bloch stood over his fifty-one-year-old son with bowed head and tears streaming down his cheeks.[18] "The Rosenberg case killed him too," he said.

(d) Gas Chamber[19]

The use of a gas chamber for execution was inspired by the use of poisonous gas in World War I as well as the popularity of the gas oven as a means of suicide. Nevada became the first state to adopt execution by lethal gas in 1924 and carried out the first execution the same year. After that it served as a means of carrying out the death sentence 31 times. Lethal gas was seen as an improvement over other forms of execution, because it was less violent and did not disfigure or mutilate the body. The last execution by lethal gas took place in Arizona in 1999.

State statutes typically and simply provide: "The punishment of death must be inflicted by the administration of a lethal gas."

The execution protocol for most states in the United States authorises the use of a steel airtight execution chamber, equipped with a chair and attached restraints. The inmate is restrained at his chest, waist, arms and ankles, and wears a mask during the execution. The chair is equipped with a metal container beneath the seat. Cyanide pellets are placed in this container. A metal canister is on the floor under the container filled with a sulphuric acid solution. There are three executioners, and each executioner turns one key. When the three keys are turned, an electric switch causes the bottom of the cyanide container to open, allowing the cyanide to fall into the sulphuric acid solution, producing a lethal gas. Unconsciousness can occur within a few seconds if the prisoner takes a deep breath. However, if he or she holds the breath, death can take much longer, and the prisoner usually goes into wild convulsions. A heart monitor attached to the inmate is read in the control room, and after the warden pronounces the inmate dead, ammonia is pumped into the execution chamber to neutralise the gas. Exhaust fans then remove the inert fumes from the chamber into two scrubbers that contain water and serve as a neutralising agent. The neutralising process takes approximately 30 minutes from the time the offender's death is determined. Death is estimated usually to occur within 6 to 18 minutes of the lethal gas emissions (see North Carolina Execution Procedures).

The most common problems encountered are the obvious agony suffered by the inmate and the length of time to cause death.

Crews wearing gas masks decontaminate the body with bleach solution, and it is out gassed before being released. If this process is not done, the undertaker or anyone handling the body would be killed. Five states in the USA authorise the use of the gas chamber as an alternative to lethal injection, viz. Arizona, California, Maryland, Missouri and Wyoming. In most cases, the prisoner is allowed to choose the method of execution. Eleven people have been executed by lethal gas in the United States since 1976. This method, however, is expensive and cumbersome. It also brings back to mind the sad fact that hundreds of thousands of Jews were killed in gas chambers by Nazi Germany.

(i) Evans – The Last Face You'll Ever See[20]

In 1981, Cannie Ray Evans was condemned to death by a Mississippi court for killing the employee of a convenience store during a robbery. On July 9, 1987 he was executed in a gas chamber.

At 12:01, Evans looked around the chamber as they strapped him in — at the crucifix on the wall, the clock to his right, the doctors behind the window to his left, and Charles Tare Rogers to the right, at the open door, and finally at Cabana, standing at the mouth. Cabana followed Connie Ray's eyes, and felt there was something horribly wrong. "I'm killing a friend of mine tonight." Then he realised that Childs and van Landingham had forgotten to draw the black drapes. The witnesses were seeing everything, all the preparations. Worse yet, he could see them. Stepping away from the chamber mouth, he asked Chaplain Padgett to spend Evans' last minutes with him. "I can't do this," he said.

A step outside the door, however, he turned and looked at Evans. He had been so brave and explicit, asking about this machine that would kill him, but his look was exactly the same who was hypersensitive to the slightest details of the numbed, impassive. Evans had turned off. This time Cabana had too. The eyes of all the witnesses were on Evans, but he wasn't there.

The red phone rang. Cabana remembered telling Evans it would happen this way. He looked at the phone, and back at Evans, who was still looking at him. Their eyes locked again, and Cabana felt himself falling into a trance as the phone sounded again. Evans' eyes were huge and full of trust and pleading and resignation. It was impossible to tear away from them. 'Mr. Cabana,' Presley said, holding out the red phone.

Presley said his name again. "I'm getting out of here," Cabana thought, suddenly aware that his heart was racing. He remembered how it had beaten the same way for Johnson. He wondered why he would inflict that horrible drumming on himself twice.

He finally took a step to his right for the telephone. Sonny's voice, telling him to go ahead, was filled with sadness. Cabana hadn't broken eye contact with Evans, and it wasn't necessary to say a word or shake his head. The only thing left was to read the paper.

Last time, he'd despised the warrant. Now his hatred the clipped sound of his voice, his fake southern accent, until the final words — "Do you wish to make a final statement?" — came out, so dispassionately.

"I do have something to say," Evans told him. His voice was calm and intimate. "But I want to say it privately to you."

Cabana took a step in, feeling the horrible repulsion of the black chair as he approached, and his warmth towards the man sitting in it. The chair was so high he didn't have to bend to get his ear to Evans's mouth. "I'm embarrassed," Evans said after thanking Cabana for his friendship. Somehow, Cabana knew

Evans wanted to offer absolution, as he'd asked for Cabana's. Didn't the condemned always absolve the warden?

This one was a dagger. "From one Christian to another," he said, "I love you. You can bet I'm going to tell the Man how good you are." Cabana reached for Evans' arm and squeezed it. Then he stepped out of the chamber, van Landingham darted in with the cyanide, and Cabana found himself next to Charles Tate Rogers as the chamber door was closed and the wheel was turned. Presley said everything was ready, and Cabana looked at the chemical room door, where Hocutt and Parker stood with their arms folded. Cabana could tell Hocutt was wondering why he'd gotten so involved, and he knew Hocutt was right. There was no point in it.

Rogers didn't throw the lever. He was looking at Cabana. 'Do it,' Cabana said, to no one in particular as he looked back at Evans. His mouth formed the words I love you, too. Rogers looked at him quizzically. Apparently, Cabana hadn't said 'Do it' out loud.

'Do it,' he screamed. The lever dropped with its grating noise, and Rogers shouted the time to Ronnie Fulcher, whom Hocutt had asked to be the log keeper. Evans breathed quickly several times, and then held his breath while the cloud hit his face. His fingers squeezed the edge of the chair, his lips pursed to slits, and his eyes darkened with the effort. Whatever part of his brain had turned off was back on now fighting. The thin muscles of his neck stood out.

'Jesus Christ,' Cabana screamed, startling everyone. "Make him breathe!" Evans' lips opened for three quick, involuntary gasps, and he was on his way. It took fifteen minutes for his heart to stop; death seemed to go a lot harder than Johnson's; more seething, eye rolling and horrible rippling of the muscles, an even louder gaseous groan halfway through. A compulsive exerciser and health food fanatic, Evans was in superb physical condition.

Hocutt had decided Evans would be hosed down while he was inside the chamber, rather than on the table in the last night cell. Cabana watched Sergeant Cook and an assistant do the hosing, and then he joined Hocutt in signing the death certificate on the coroner's jury. It was 1 a.m. before he left the death house for the press conference in the administration building.

Cabana's wife, Miriam had spent the night packing the car and was waiting at the wheel outside the administration building. They were headed for a few weeks' vacation with the kids later that morning, their first since coming to Parchman. 'No more,' Cabana said, shaking his head to Miriam before walking in to do the press conference. "I don't want to do this anymore."

He was talking about Connie Ray Evans and executions, but as he said it, he realised he was through with prisons. Something had broken inside him, and he'd never been able to put it back together. Eight months later, he would leave Parchman to run a media security facility in southern Mississippi. Three years later, he be out entirely, getting his doctorate and teaching criminology at Hattiesburg, travelling across the country as a leading abolitionist: consulting speaking and testifying as an expert witness. In twenty years of prison work, Cabana had never questioned his own authority, his own correctness. It had always seemed true by definition. Evans' final moments had stripped him of that claim. He would have titles but no substance.

At the press conference, everyone wanted to know what Evans had whispered in the chambers. He refused to say. After a long silence, they asked about his mood. "As well as can be expected," he said, "given the circumstances." With nothing left they asked about Evans' last meal, and he gave them the menu, and "he remarked that he was particularly appreciative of chocolates and cake." The last reporter left at 2 a.m. and Cabana and Dwight Presley locked the building up behind them. The moon was high and brilliant, and the two men looked at it before Cabana opened the passenger door and got in with Mariam. Presley asked him what he was going to do.

"I think I'm going to call my mother."

There is a very, very thin line between the executioner and the executed.

(ii) Visitor to Jimmy Lee Gray's Grave – Story of the Executioner

Colonel Hocutt was the chief executioner of a gas chamber in Mississippi for twenty years. He reluctantly offered to take me on a tour of Jimmy Lee Gray's grave outside Indianola, half an hour down 49W. Several times this morning, he's tried to talk me out of going, and then just as quickly talked himself back into it. Twelve years have passed since Jimmy Lee Gray was executed in Parchman's gas chamber, but people keep asking for a tour of the grave from Hocutt, who mixed the sulphuric acid bath that dissolved the cyanide that killed Gray. He usually takes the people who ask, though he says there's nothing to see, "They always spend a lot of time by his stone, for reasons I cannot fathom," he tells me. "No one except the lawyers, church ladies, and the death penalty opponents took any interest in Jimmy Lee Gray while he was alive. People on death row get a lot of mail, you'd be surprised, but he didn't. His family never visited, and his victims' families didn't show up for his asphyxiation. Even the guys on the row didn't want to know nothing about him, and they're so low, they wanted to see a centipede shit."

Gray was famous enough afterwards. He took a long time to die or so most of the witnesses to his asphyxiation claimed. A doctor monitoring his heartbeat on a remote said he was clinically dead and took two minutes for his execution, but his head banged back repeatedly on a ventilation pipe behind the chair in the chamber. But the legend has grown that his death was a ten-minute torture. It was the first time in nineteen years that the gas chamber had been used, and it was the beginning of the end for it. By turn, Hocutt says he believes the doctor's assessment of a quick death and that he truly doesn't care.

"I could have sat on Jimmy Lee and ate a sandwich while he asphyxiated." He tells me. "It wasn't pretty. The fact that had been bungled reflected badly on the State of Mississippi, but Jimmy Lee Gray was a piece of shit. He took a three-year-old girl into a logging woods outside Pascagoula, raped her, sodomised her, pushed her face into a bog by a drainage ditch until she choked on mud, then threw her body off a bridge into a stream. As far as I'm concerned, Jimmy Lee Gray died too painlessly..." On returning Hotcutt said, "No son tells his father he wishes to become an executioner. They just become, as I did."

(e) Lethal Injection[21]

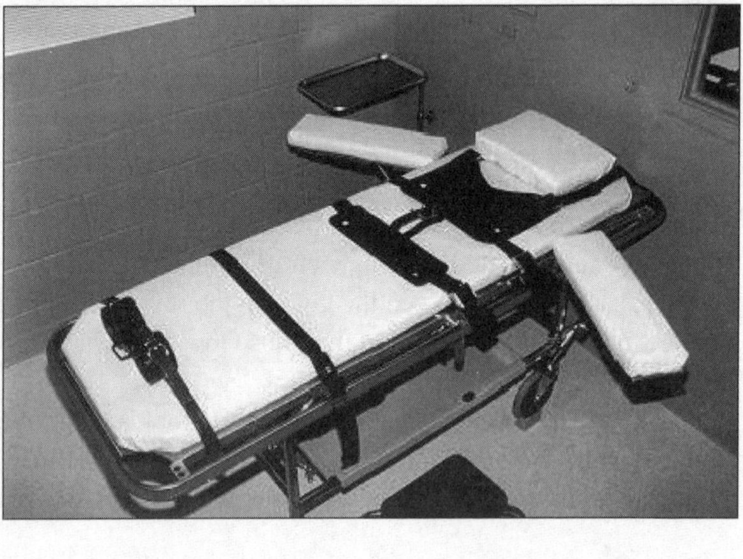

Lethal injection was first considered as a means of execution in 1888 when New York's J. Mount Bleyer, MD, put it forward in an article in the Medico-Legal Journal suggesting that an intravenous injection of six grains of Morphine should be used for execution of death sentence. The idea did not catch on and New York introduced the electric chair instead (based on the findings of the New York Commission of Inquiry 1888). It was again put forward in 1977 by Dr. Stanley Deutsch, who at the time chaired the Anesthesiology Department of Oklahoma University Medical School.

In response to a call by Oklahoma State Senator Bill Dawson for a cheaper alternative to repairing the State's derelict electric chair, Deutsch described a way to administer drugs through an intravenous drip so as to cause death rapidly and without pain. Deutsch wrote to Senator Bill Dawson, "Having been anaesthetised on several occasions with ultrashort-acting barbiturates and having administered these drugs for approximately 20 years, I can assure you that this is a rapid, pleasant way of producing unconsciousness." And Oklahoma thus became the first State in the USA to legislate for it in 1977. Texas introduced a similar legislation later the same year to replace electric chair and carried out the first execution by the method of lethal injection on December 7, 1982 when Charles Brooks was put to death for murder. The procedure began at 12.07 a.m. He was certified dead at 12.16 a.m. There was no apparent problem and Brooks seemed to die quite easily. At first he raised his head, clenched his fist and seemed to yawn or gasp before passing into unconsciousness.

State statutes typically provide: "The punishment of death must be inflicted by continuous, intravenous administration of a lethal quantity of an ultrashort-acting barbiturate in combination with a chemical paralytic agent until death is pronounced by a licensed physician according to accepted standards of medical practice."[22]

Despite some variation, the administration of lethal injection procedure is generally uniform in most states. This procedure uses a combination of three drugs. The first, sodium thiopental or sodium pentothal, is a barbiturate that renders the prisoner unconscious. The second, pancuronium bromide, is a muscle relaxant that paralyses the diaphragm and lungs. The third, potassium chloride, causes cardiac arrest. Each chemical is lethal in the amounts administered.

Lethal injection protocols vary from State to State. Typically, the prisoner is strapped to a gurney (which is a wheeled-hospital style trolley bed) or a fixed execution table rather like an operating theatre table by leather or webbing straps over the body and legs. His bare arms are strapped to boards projecting from the sides of the gurney. Trained technicians then insert a catheter into a vein in each arm, a process that sounds much simpler than it often is. Once the catheters are in place, tubes carrying saline solution are connected to the catheter ends and the prisoner is either wheeled into the execution chamber or the curtains surrounding it are drawn back to allow the witnesses to see the procedure. When the condemned person has made a final statement, if any, the prison warden gives the signal for the execution to begin and the technician(s), hidden from view behind a two-way mirror begins to manually inject the three chemicals comprising typically 15-50 cc of Sodium thiopental, 15-50 cc of Pavulon (the generic name for Pancuronium bromide) and 15-50 cc of Potassium chloride.

There is a short interval between each chemical during which saline solution is injected to clean the vein and prevent any chemical reaction which could block it. Typically, the actual injections will take from three to five minutes to complete.

Sodium thiopental is a short-acting barbiturate which causes unconsciousness quite quickly. Pavulon is a muscle relaxant that paralyses the diaphragm and thus arrests breathing whilst Potassium chloride finishes the job by causing cardiac arrest. In most cases, the prisoner is unconscious in about a minute after the Sodium thiopental has been injected and is dead in around eight minutes, with no obvious signs of physical suffering. In some States, a fully automated lethal injection machine is used that runs off a 12-volt battery. It injects the chemicals in the right order and amount once the catheters are in place. The machine has six syringes activated by mechanical plungers. Three syringes hold the lethal drugs and the other three contain harmless saline solution. Two buttons control the machine, one for the lethal syringes and one for the identical looking harmless ones. The two executioners each press a button and the syringes release the drugs into the vein. The condemned prisoner thus is put to death while in sleep by this swift and painless method. But the identity of who is the real executioner is kept secret even from the person who administers the lethal dose as to avoid trauma.

The most common problem encountered is collapsing veins and the inability to properly insert the injection. Some States allow for a Thorazine or sedative injection to facilitate insertion of the injection needle.

The Philippines has also started using lethal injection for executions replacing the electric chair. It carried out its first such execution when Leo Echegaray was put to death for child rape on February 4, 1999. Six more men had been executed by this method by the end of 2000. Guatemala also switched to lethal injection after a botched firing squad execution in 1996 and has carried out three executions since then. China also has been experimenting with lethal injection, although most executions continue to be by shooting. The present trend thus seems to favour execution by lethal injection. This method so far is the best mode of extinguishing life. First the inmate is made unconscious and then a lethal dose is administered and he dies in sleep. It involves no mutilation of the body or pain, except for the prick of the needle.

(i) Controversial Execution of Troy Davis 2011[23]

International outcry can't save convicted man: Troy Davis defiant till the time of lethal injection: 22 years of politics over race and death penalty sees closure

Proclaiming his innocence, Troy Davis was put to death by lethal injection, his life — and the hopes of supporters worldwide — prolonged by several hours while the US Supreme Court reviewed and then declined to act on a petition from his lawyers to stay the execution.

Thousands of appeals for clemency were made including by legal novelist John Grisham. Rev. Al Sharpton led the demonstration outside the execution premises in Georgia. Several activists said that his execution should give a wake up call to US politicians to abolish capital punishment because of the controversial nature of the case.

Davis, 42, was convicted in 1991 for murdering Mark MacPhail, a police officer in Savannah, Georgia, in 1989. MacPhail had rushed to help a homeless man who was being assaulted by a group that included Davis when he was shot in the face and heart.

In 2007, Davis prepared for his final hours, but the state parole board stayed the execution until its members were "convinced that there is no doubt as to the guilt of the accused." In 2008, 90 minutes before the execution, the Supreme Court stepped in, but ultimately did not hear the case. On September 22, 2011, his last-ditch appeal to the Supreme Court delayed the execution by four hours, but it was rejected. He entered the death chamber shortly before 11 p.m., four hours after the scheduled time. He died at 11.08 p.m.

This final chapter before his execution has become an international symbol of the battle over the death penalty and racial imbalance in the justice system. "It harkens back to some ugly days in the history of Georgia State," said the Rev. Raphael Warnock of the Ebenezer Baptist Church, who visited Davis two days before his execution.

Davis remained defiant till the end, said reporters who witnessed his death. He looked directly at the members of the family of Mark MacPhail, the officer he was convicted of killing, and told them they had the wrong man.

"I did not personally kill your son, father, brother," he said. "All I can ask is that you look deeper into this case, so you really can finally see the truth." He is also supposed to have said that he did not have a gun. He told his supporters and family to 'keep the faith', and to prison personnel, "May God have mercy on your souls; may God bless your souls."

For Davis' family and other supporters gathered in front of the prison, the final hours were mixed with hope, tears and exhaustion. The crowd was buoyed by the Supreme Court's involvement, but crushed when it issued a one-sentence refusal to consider a stay.

When news of his death came, the family left quietly. Davis' body was driven out of the grounds about midnight.The appeal to the Supreme Court was one of several last-ditch efforts by Davis on September 22. Earlier in the day, Edward O DuBose, President of the Georgia chapter of the National Association for the Advancement of Colored People (NAACP), said that the vote by the Georgia parole board — 3 to 2 — to deny clemency to Davis was so close that he had hoped Davis might be saved from execution. Davis' supporters also attempted to reach out to the original judge to rescind the death order, and to plead with President Barack Obama for a reprieve. The case, which was a slow and convoluted exercise in legal maneuvering and death penalty politics, saw over 630,000 petitions seeking a stay on the execution.

Among those asking for clemency were former President Jimmy Carter, Archbishop Desmond Tutu, and 51 members of the Congress.

(ii) First Person Report of Davis' Execution by Greg Bluestein

"He blinked and squeezed his eyes and curtain closed."

I have covered about 10 executions in Georgia. None of them are easy. This was by far the most unusual.

There were four reporters besides me. We ended up waiting for more than four hours in a somber prison break room. We made small talk and speculated about whether the Supreme Court would intervene.

Around 10.30 p.m., a guard walked in. ‘You ready?’

We were led into a white van and delivered to the squat white building on the edge of the prison that serves as the death chamber. We watched the slain officer’s son. Mark MacPhail Jr. entered. Behind him, Jason Ewart, the condemned man’s attorney walked in. A country coroner’s van rolled up.

By the time we were inside, officials had strapped Davis to the gurney. There was a glass window with a curtain separating Davis from the witnesses, who sat in three rows of seats. There were about 20 of us.

Davis searched for Ewart, who nodded slightly when they locked eyes. MacPhail Jr., sitting in the front row, focused on Davis.

When it was time to deliver his last words, Davis seized the moment, speaking quickly and confidently.

He told the MacPhail family he was not responsible for the death. “I am innocent. The incident that happened that night is not my fault,” he said.

Davis blinked his eyes rapidly. He squeezed them tight. The curtain closed.

Chart giving a Glance of Comparative Analysis of Present Mode of Executing Death Sentence[24]

Hanging by Neck Till Death	Shooting	Gas Chamber	Electrocution Injection	Intravenous Lethal
Simple to execute	Simple to execute	Simple to execute	Simple to execute	Simple to execute
Execution process takes more than 40 minutes to declare prisoner to be dead	Execution process takes not more than few minutes to declare prisoner to be dead	Not more than 2 minutes	More than 20 minutes	Execution process takes 5 to 9 minutes to declare prisoner dead
Less scientific equipments are required	Less scientific equipments are required	More scientific but complicated equipment required	easily available	More scientific equipments are required but they are
Uncertainty as to time required for the prisoner to become unconscious	Instant death	Not always instantaneous death	Not instantaneous death	Unconsciousness takes place immediately after the application of anesthesia and dies in sleep
May cause lingering death	Instant death	Sometimes lingering death	Lingering death	Not a lingering death

Most of the time may involve enormous pain	Pain may hardly be involved	Suffocation	Intense pain involved	Pain only as a result of needle prick
Has been abandoned by most countries considering it not to be civilised	Most countries provide for the option of either lethal injection or shooting	Only few states in the US provide for it	Popular in twentieth century, but on the way out	It is being accepted now to be the most civilised mode of execution of death sentence
Mutilation involved	Less mutilation involved	No mutilation	Severe mutilation	No mutilation involved
Not a controlled way of execution. It depends on various factors	It is always under control and does not depend on factors like physique, etc. of the convict	It is always under control	It is under control	It is the best controlled way of execution
Not generally swift	It is comparatively swift and painless	It is not always swift	Not swift and always painful	It is a painless and swift method of execution

□

4

Situation of Death Penalty and Moratorium in the World[1]

Vast majority of democratic countries of Europe and Latin America have abolished the death penalty over the last 50 years. However, it has been retained by totalitarian countries plus democracies like the United States of America and India.

Punishment of death penalty varies greatly worldwide for crimes such as murder, terrorism and narcotic trafficking to even theft. Under military laws, Court Martial inflicts capital sentence also for treason, desertion, mutiny, etc.

Map as on February 2011[2]

Colour scheme:

- **Blue:** Abolished for all crimes
- **Yellow-Green:** Abolished for crimes except those committed
  in exceptional circumstances (e.g. crimes committed in times of war)
- **Orange:** Abolished in practice
- **Reddish-brown:** Legal form of punishment for heinous offences. Of the 'reddish-brown' states, China is the only one that has a broad range of capital crimes, including tax fraud, minor drug offences and violent theft.

Death penalty is allowed only in six industrialized democracies, viz. India, Israel, Japan, South Korea, Singapore and the United States of America. In the USA, it was abolished in 1974, but reinstated in 1976 by some States.

Ever since the adoption of the Charter on Human Rights by the United Nations on December 10, 1948, movement towards abolition of death sentence, and/or reduction of offences for which it can be imposed is gathering force. As a result, offences for which death penalty can be given is getting progressively reduced. The period from the end of 20th century to 2011 has witnessed a growing movement for acceptance by the UN members at least for a moratorium on death punishment by countries which have it.

(a) UN Resolutions on Death Penalty[3]

International Covenant on Civil and Political Rights (ICCPR).

This resolution was adopted by the UN General Assembly on December 16, 1966 and came into force on March 23, 1976.

Relevant clauses of Article 6 which deal with death penalty read as follows:

- Every human being has the inherent right to life. This right shall be protected by law. No one shall be arbitrarily deprived of his life.
- In countries which have not abolished the death penalty, sentence of death may be imposed only for the most serious crimes in accordance with the law in force at the time of the commission of the crime…This penalty can only be carried out pursuant to a final judgement rendered by a competent court.
- Anyone sentenced to death shall have the right to seek pardon or commutation of the sentence. Amnesty, pardon or commutation of the sentence of death may be granted in all cases.
- Sentence of death shall not be imposed for crimes committed by persons below eighteen years of age and shall not be carried out on pregnant women.
- Nothing in this article shall be invoked or to prevent the abolition of capital punishment by any State Party to the present Covenant.

Article 7

No one shall be subjected to torture or to cruel, inhuman or degrading treatment or punishment. In particular, no one shall be subjected without his free consent to medical or scientific experimentation.

The Human Rights Committee has, however, found violations of Article 7 in certain cases concerning detention on death row, the method of execution, and the issuance of execution warrants to mentally incapable persons.

Article 14

Article 14 requires the State parties to impose death

punishment pursuant to a final judgement rendered by a competent and independent court after a fair trial. There should be presumption of innocence, the minimum guarantees for the defence and the right to review by a higher tribunal.

Article 2 of Charter of the European Union prohibits the use of capital punishment.

On May 25, 1984, the United Nations Economic and Social Council (ECOSOC) provided standards and safeguards guaranteeing protection of the rights of those facing the death penalty, viz. its Resolution 1984/50, annex. General Assembly Resolution 29/118, 1984 which states that one of the important standards and safeguards against the death penalty as is enunciated in Safeguard No. 9, "Where capital punishment occurs, it shall be carried out so as to inflict minimum possible suffering."

On May 29, 1998, United Kingdom voted for the Protocol of European Convention of Human Rights. This means that it cannot reintroduce capital punishment unless it withdraws from the Council of Europe.

On December 15, 1989, the UN adopted the Second Optional Protocol to the ICCPR, which abolishes death penalty during peacetime. This protocol came into force on July 11, 1991.

On November 20, 1989, the UN General Assembly passed the Resolution on the Convention on the Rights of the Child which came into force on September 2, 1990 and is binding under Article 37 of ICCPR. It reminded the members not to execute a person below 18 years of age.

The ECOSOC Safeguards Resolution of 2004 again reminded the members of the UN to conform to the requirement of Article 14 of the ICCPR in imposing death penalty.

Protocol 13 of the European Convention, which came into force on May 3, 2002, called for complete abolition of death penalty. As of 2011, a majority of the countries including members of the European Union have ratified it. Armenia and Poland have signed the protocol but not ratified it. Russia and Azerbaijan, however, have not signed it.

(b) UN Resolutions on Moratorium on Death Punishment[4]

Italy in 1980s took the initiative in the United Nations in passing a resolution on a moratorium on death punishment by countries which have not abolished it and to promote and strengthen the growing trends towards elimination of death penalty. Interestingly, five million appeals were made to the United Nations for abolishing it.

On November 15, 2007, the Third Committee of the UN General Assembly passed a non-binding resolution for a global moratorium on execution which states: "There is no conclusive evidence of the death penalty's deterrent value and that any miscarriage or failure of justice in the death penalty's implementation is irreversible and irreparable."

The resolution welcomed "the decisions taken by an increasing number of States to apply a moratorium on executions, followed in many cases by the abolition of the death penalty", and expressed deep concern that the death penalty continues to be applied in some countries.

It called on nations that do impose the death penalty to ensure they meet internationally agreed minimum standards on the safeguards for those facing execution, and to provide the United Nations Secretary-General with information about their use of capital punishment and observation of the safeguards.

Further, the resolution asked countries to progressively

restrict the use of the death penalty such as by reducing the number of offences for which it may be imposed, and calls on those States that have abolished the practice to not reintroduce it.

This resolution was passed by 99 to 52 with 33 abstentions.

On December 18, 2007, the UN General Assembly again passed a non-binding resolution calling for a worldwide moratorium on the death penalty, with the ultimate aim of abolishing capital punishment. This time 104, i.e. five more countries voted in favour and 54 against with 29 abstentions. It may be noted that United States, China, India, Indonesia, Iran and Syria opposed the moratorium. Furthermore, after terrorism, Sri Lanka and Jamaica ended the moratorium on death punishment.

On December 18, 2008 and again on December 21, 2010, the General Assembly adopted resolutions giving calls for a global moratorium on capital punishment. Voting was respectively 106 to 46 with 34 abstentions and 109 to 41 with 35 abstentions.

The Parliamentary Assembly of the Council of Europe has also been lobbying against those countries which allow executions to have at least a moratorium on death punishment.

This trend shows that more and more countries are voting for a moratorium on capital punishment and the countries abolishing it is also increasing.

It is important to realise that capital crimes vary greatly around the world. In some States of the US, the death penalty is restricted to multiple murders or murder with aggravated circumstances. In India, it is restricted to cases when murder is premeditated and brutal. Engaging in pre-marital sex, changing one's religion, same-gender sexual behaviour and adultery are capital offences in some predominately Muslim countries.

Death punishment for drug-related offences exists in Afghanistan; Bangladesh; Brunei; China;. Egypt; Indonesia; Iran; Iraq; Kuwait; Laos; Malaysia; Oman; Pakistan; Saudi Arabia; Singapore; Somalia; Sri Lanka; Thailand; Vietnam; United Arab Emirates; United States and Zimbabwe.[5] The Supreme Court of India in 2011 suggested that death punishment should be imposed for second offence of mass drug trafficking.

In 2007, 51 countries had death penalty on their statute books as compared to 60 countries in 2004.

(c) Death Penalty Country-wise[6]

By 2011, a large number of countries had abolished death penalty, but it was permitted for exceptional crimes such as crimes committed under military law or in war time including treason and espionage.

(i) The names of these countries alongwith year of their abolishing it are given below:

Albania (2000); Andorra (1990); Angola (1992); Argentina (2008); Armenia (2003); Australia (1984); Austria (1950); Azerbaijan (1998); Belgium (1996); Bhutan (2004); Bosnia-Herzegovina (1997); Bulgaria (1998); Cambodia (1989); Canada (1976); Cape Verde (1981); Chile (2008); Colombia (1910); Cook Islands (2007); Costa Rica (1977); Côte d'Ivoire (2000); Croatia (1990); Cyprus (1983); Czech Republic (1990); Denmark (1933); Djibouti (1995); Dominican Republic (1966); East Timor (1999); Ecuador (1906); Estonia (1998); Finland (1949); France (1981); Georgia (1997); Germany (1949); Greece (1993); Guinea-Bissau (1993); Haiti (1987); Honduras (1956); Hungary (1990); Iceland (1928); Ireland (1990); Italy (1947); Kiribati (1979; Liberia (2005); Liechtenstein (1987); Lithuania (1998); Luxembourg (1979); Macedonia (1991); Malta (1971); Marshall Islands (1986); Mauritius (1995);

Mexico (2005); Micronesia (1986); Moldova (1995); Monaco (1962); Montenegro (2002); Mozambique (1990); Namibia (1990); Nepal (1990); Netherlands (1970); New Zealand (1961); Nicaragua (1979); Niue (N.A.); Norway (1905); Palau (N.A.); Panama (1903); Paraguay (1992); Poland (1997); Portugal (1967); Philippines (2006); Romania (1989); Rwanda (2007); Samoa (2004); San Marino (1848); São Tomé and Príncipe (1990); Senegal (2004); Serbia (2002); Seychelles (1993); Slovak Republic (1990); Slovenia (1989); Solomon Islands (1966); South Africa (1995); Spain (1978); Sweden (1921); Switzerland (1942); Turkey (2002); Turkmenistan (1999); Tuvalu (1978); Ukraine (1999); United Kingdom (1973); Uruguay (1907); Uzbekistan (2008); Vanuatu (1980); Vatican City (1969); Venezuela (1963).

(ii) Death penalty exists in the following countries:

Afghanistan; Antigua and Barbuda; Bahamas; Bahrain; Bangladesh; Barbados; Belarus; Belize; Botswana; Burundi; Cameroon; Chad; China (People's Republic); Comoros; Congo (Democratic Republic); Cuba; Dominica; Egypt; Equatorial Guinea; Eritrea; Ethiopia; Gabon; Ghana; Guatemala; Guinea; Guyana; India; Indonesia; Iran; Iraq; Israel, Jamaica; Japan; Jordan; Korea (North); Korea (South); Kuwait; Laos; Lebanon; Lesotho; Libya; Malawi; Malaysia; Mongolia; Nigeria; Oman; Pakistan; Palestinian Authority; Qatar; St. Kitts and Nevis; St. Lucia; St. Vincent and the Grenadines; Saudi Arabia; Sierra Leone; Singapore; Somalia; Sudan; Swaziland; Syria; Taiwan; Tajikistan; Tanzania; Thailand; Trinidad and Tobago; Uganda; United Arab Emirates; United States; Vietnam; Yemen; Zambia; Zimbabwe.

Although more countries have abolished the death penalty, sixty percent of the world's population lives in countries which enforce it.

Countries that have Executed People during 2011[7]

In the year 2003, China executed 200 persons, Iran 139 persons, Saudi Arabia 79 and the US executed 66 persons.

In the year 2007, the following countries carried out 25 or more executions: Iraq 29 persons; Iran 265; Pakistan 29; Saudi Arabia 156; and the US 42.

Countries with 2 to 25 executions were: Afghanistan 15 persons; Bangladesh 6; China 13; India 10; Japan 9; North Korea 8; Singapore 2; Somalia 3; Sudan 2; Syria 5; and Yemen 7 persons.

Countries with one execution each were: Belarus, Botswana, Ethiopia, Indonesia and Kuwait.

Most countries use mercifully quick methods of killing prisoners. Techniques include hanging victims by first allowing them to free-fall until the rope breaks their neck and kills them, shooting, beheading, lethal injection and the electric chair.

Only a few predominately Muslim countries are known to execute prisoners by torturing them to death. In Iran, a method that is often used in public hangings involves hoisting the prisoner in the air or removing a box that they are standing on until they eventually strangle to death. Estimates of the number of stoning in Iran alone vary from two to many hundreds during 2007. Here the victim is immobilised by having their bodies buried up to their neck. They are then pelted with stones until they die. The stones are carefully chosen so that they are large enough to inflict considerable damage and pain, yet not large enough to kill the person quickly.

Russia retains capital punishment statutes but has not executed criminals for many years. It executed its last prisoner in 1996. In 2010, Russia accepted the resolution on moratorium on death punishment, but Duma (its supreme legislative body) refused to ratify it.

Kenya executed its last prisoner in 1984. The Government of Kenya had planned to abolish the death penalty in the country by mid-2003, but took no action.

Taiwan's Parliament studied the abolition of the death penalty in 2004 but took no action. The government has proposed abolition, but not implemented it because 80% of public opinion favours executions. The number of executions has, however, dropped from 32 in 1998 to 3 in 2004 and 2005, and none in 2007.

While courts in 67 countries handed down death sentences in 2010, only 23 countries actually carried out executions.[8]

□

5

Situation and Methods of Death Punishment in the United States of America[1]

At present, in the United States of America, the following States have no death penalty: Alaska, Hawaii, North Dakota, Minesota, Wisconsin, Iowa, Michigan, Maine, Vermont, Massasachusetts, Rhode Island, New Hampshire, New Jersey, West Virginia, New Mexico, Illinois and District of Columbia. It may be mentioned that Michigan was the first State to abolish death penalty as early as 1846.

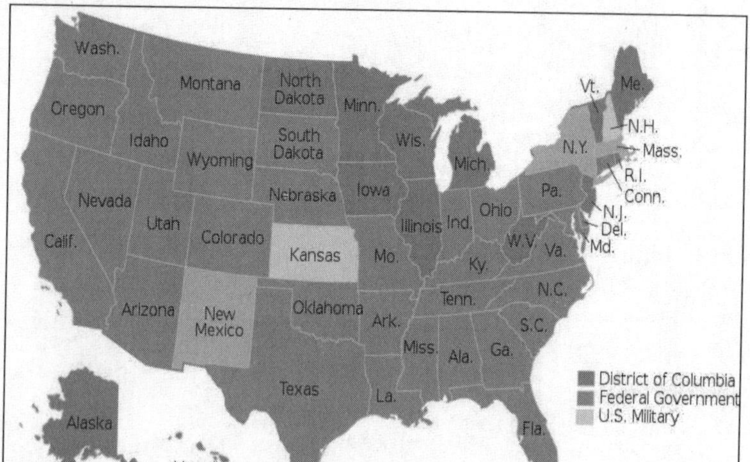

Notes:

- **Blue** states have no death penalty statute.
- **Yellow-green** states have a death penalty statute but have not executed anyone since 1976.
- **Reddish-orange** states have executed people since 1976.
- The Kansas Supreme Court declared that the death penalty
  is constitutional by a 5-4 vote on June 26, 2006.
- New Jersey abolished the death penalty on December 18, 2007 — the first state in 40 years to do so.
- Illinois abolished the death penalty on March 9, 2011.
- Nebraska has death penalty by lethal injection, but the State Supreme Court invalidated it in 2011.

Stay of All Executions

By the the land mark judgement of Supreme Court, *Furman* vs. *Georgia* 408 US 230 (1972), the Supreme Court of US stayed all executions. However in 1976 as many as 37 states reinstated death punishment, though statistics show that there are more murders in states having death punishment than those not having it.

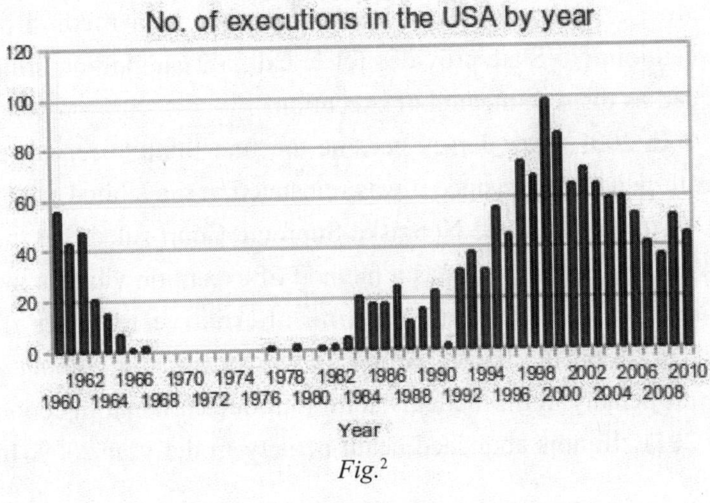

Fig.[2]

Persons in Death Row: Government (59); Military (7)
Executions: Government (3); Military (0)
Gender (Male): Government (1); Military (0)
Gender (Female): Government (0); Military (0)
ETHNICITY:
Black: Government (31); Military (5)
White: Government (23); Military (1)
Latino: Government (23); Military (1)
Asian: Government (0); Military (1)
Native: Government (1); Military (0)

(I) Methods of Execution in States

In the United States, five different methods of execution are prescribed in the 37 States and the Federal Government that currently have death penalty. These methods are: lethal injection, electrocution, lethal gas, firing squad and hanging. The vast majority of States provide for execution by lethal injection. Twenty States provide for alternative methods of execution, contingent upon the choice of the inmate. Only one State i.e. Nebraska have lethal injection as a method of execution. No State provides for lethal gas, hanging or firing squad as the sole method of execution.[3]

In 2007, New Jersey became the first State to repeal its death penalty laws since it was reinstated in the United States in 1976. In 2008, the Nebraska Supreme Court ruled that the use of the electric chair as a method of execution violates the Nebraska Constitution. With no alternative methods of execution on the books, Nebraska was practically without a death penalty untill the legislature introducted lethal injection in 2011. Illinois abolished death penalty in the year 2009. In

Kansas, death punishment has been abolished and lethal injection is used only by the Federal Government.[4]

(a) Lethal Injection

Alabama; Arizona; Arkansas; California; Colorado; Connecticut; Delaware; Florida; Georgia; Idaho; Indiana; Kansas; Kentucky; Louisiana; Maryland; Mississippi; Missouri; Montana; Nebraska; Nevada; New Hampshire; New Mexico; New York; North Carolina; Ohio; Oklahoma; Oregon; Pennsylvania; South Carolina; South Dakota; Tennessee; Texas; Utah; Virginia; Oklahoma; Oregon; Washington; Wyoming; and the Federal Government.

(b) Electrocution

Alabama; Arkansas; Florida; Kentucky; Oklahoma; South Carolina; Tennessee; and Virginia.

(c) Lethal Gas

Arizona; California; Missouri; and Wyoming

(d) Firing Squad

Idaho; Oklahoma; and Utah

(e) Hanging

Delaware, New Hampshire; and Washington

The following States give a choice to the inmates as to the method of execution. But if the inmate does not give any choice, the first method is used.

1. Alabama — Lethal Injection or Electrocution
2. California — Lethal Injection or Gas
3. Florida — Lethal Injection or Electrocution
4. Idaho — Lethal Injection or Firing Squad

5. Ohio — Electrocution or Lethal Injection
6. South Carolina — Lethal Injection or Electrocution
7. Utah — Firing Squad or Lethal Injection
8. Virginia — Lethal Injection or Electrocution
9. Washington — Hanging or Lethal Injection
10. Federal Govt. — Lethal Injection or State Methods

According to Gallup Poll, from 1976 to November 2011, 2,811 persons were executed, of which 103 were by lethal injection, 157 by electrocution, 11 by gas chamber and 3 each by hanging and firing squad.

Since 1976, 34 per cent black Americans were executed, while their population is about 12 per cent. Women accounted for 9 per cent of those executed.

Since 1976, 137 death punishment convicts waived their right to appeal, and in the States of Connecticut, Oregon, Florida and Dakota. Death punishment convicts volunteered for execution.

Since 1976, it is estimated that 139 innocent persons were executed and the executioner Timothy Davis of 2011 is supposed to be the last one.

In 2010, there were 3,260 death row inmates, out of which 61 were females.

It is significant to note that the suicide rate among death row inmates is double that of the American population.[6]

(II) Public Opinion about Death Penalty[7]

Public Opinion in 2011

Death Penalty for murder	61% in favour	35% against	4% No opinion
Death Penalty for murder	65% morally acceptable	28% morally wrong	7% No opinion

Death Penalty for murder	49% death penalty	46% life imprisonment with no parole	5% No opinion
Death Penalty for murder	32% deterrent	64% No deterrent	4% No opinion
Death Penalty for murder	52% applied fairly	41% not fairly	7% No opinion
In the last five opinion years, death penalty was imposed	59% on innocent	31% on guilty	10% No opinion

Public Opinion in 2003

In 2003, those who opposed death penalty, 41% felt it was wrong to take life; 25% felt they were wrongly convicted; 4% were of the opinion that it did not deter murder; 4% felt there was unfair application, 68% favoured death penalty.

Public Opinion in 2002

Death Penalty for women	68% in favour	29% opposed	3% No opinion
Death Penalty for mentally retarded	13% in favour	82% opposed	5% No opinion
Death Penalty	28 % in favour for juvenile	69% opposed	3% No opinion
Death Penalty	70 % in favour by men	24% opposed	6% No opinion
Death Penalty	58% in favour by men	36% opposed	6% No opinion
Death Penalty by whites	69% in favour	26% opposed	5% No opinion
Death Penalty by non-whites	55% in favour	37% opposed	8% No opinion

But in case of Timothy McVeigh, who killed 164 persons in 2001, 80% supported death penalty.

Since 1976, when death punishment was again started in the US and upto January 1, 2012:

1,277 were executed, of which 12 were females and as many as 3,200 people were in the death row.

Executions held in 34 States:

1,203 (86.4% by lethal injection); 157 (12.3% by electrocution); 11 (0.87% by gas chamber; 3 (0.2% by hanging); 3 (0.2% by firing squad).

Texas has the highest number of executions, i.e. 474 (37%).

(III) Federal Execution[8]

In the USA, the State judiciary has the final jurisdiction in the criminal judicial system. However, in case of assassination having national repercussions like those of President John F. Kennedy and Martin Luther King and recently murders by bombers, the jurisdiction is vested in the Federal Courts.

In case of execution under Federal Law, the American Federal Bureau of Prisons has lethal injection facility at the federal prison in Terre Haute, Indiana. The death house is located inside a non-descript brick building outside the main penitentiary compound, and consists of five viewing rooms surrounding the execution chamber. The chamber is a stark, hospital-like room lined with green tiles and bare except for the large gurney equipped with five velcro restrains and a sink in one corner. The intravenous tubes pass through a small opening in the wall and into the executioner's room nearby. All but one room, the executioner's, are equipped with large two-way windows with curtains. The executioner's room is fitted with one-way glass. During an execution, prison officials maintain an open telephone line to the Justice Department in Washington as the President of the USA has the sole authority to grant last-minute clemency. Overhead, a camera linked to a monitor inside the executioner's room keeps tabs on the process to note whether the prisoner suffers any pain during the procedure. On June 11, 2001, Timothy McVeigh, the Oklahoma City bomber, executed was under Federal law. He had placed a bomb outside the Alfred P. Murrah Federal Building, killing 168 people and injuring 850. The intravenous drip that delivered the lethal chemicals went to a catheter in McVeigh's right leg. The first drug was administered at 8.10 a.m., with the second being given at 8.11 and the final one at 8.13 and he was pronounced dead at 8.14 a.m. The whole process took only four minutes. On June 19, Juan Raul Garza, a Mexican-American drug lord, with murder record, was executed on the same gurney. The American military has also shifted to lethal injection (from hanging) and now has a facility in the basement of the military prison at Ft. Leavenworth, Kansas.

At present, crimes subject to the death penalty vary by States. All States that use capital punishment designate the highest grade of murder a capital crime, although most jurisdictions require aggravating circumstances. Treason against the United States, as well as treason against the States of Arkansas, California, Colorado, Georgia, Louisiana, Mississippi, Missouri and Washington are capital offences. Other capital crimes include the use of a weapon of mass destruction resulting in death, espionage, terrorism, certain violations of the Geneva Conventions that result in the death of one or more persons.

(IV) Legal Process[9]

The legal administration of the death penalty in the United States is complex. Typically, it involves four critical steps: (1) sentencing, (2) direct review, (3) state collateral review, and (4) federal habeas corpus. Recently, a narrow and final fifth level of process — has become increasingly important. Clemency or pardon, through which the Governor or President can unilaterally reduce or abrogate a death sentence. It is an executive rather than judicial process.

(i) Direct Review[10]

If a defendant is sentenced to death at the trial level, the case then goes into a direct review. The direct review process is a typical legal appeal. An appellate court examines the record of evidence presented in the trial court and the law that the lower court applied and decides whether the decision was legally sound or not. Direct review of a capital sentencing hearing will result in one of three outcomes. If the appellate court finds that no significant legal errors occurred in the capital sentencing hearing, the appellate court will affirm the judgement. If the appellate court finds that significant legal errors did occur, then it will reverse the judgement or nullify the sentence and order a new capital sentencing hearing. Lastly, if the appellate court finds that no reasonable juror could find the defendant eligible for the death penalty, a rarity, then it will order the defendant acquitted, or not guilty, of the crime for which he/she was given the death penalty, and order him sentenced to the next most severe punishment for which the offence is eligible. About 60% survive the process of direct review intact.

(ii) Collateral Review[11]

At times when a death sentence is affirmed on direct review, it is considered final. Yet, supplemental methods to attack the judgement, though less familiar than a typical appeal, do remain. These supplemental remedies are considered collateral review, that is, an avenue for upsetting judgements that have become otherwise final. Where the prisoner received his death sentence in a state-level trial, as is usually the case, the first step in collateral review is state collateral review. (If the case is a federal death penalty case, it proceeds immediately from direct review to federal habeas corpus.) Although all states have some type of collateral review, the process varies widely from State to State. Generally, the purpose of these collateral proceedings is to permit the prisoner to challenge his sentence on grounds that could not have been raised reasonably at trial or in direct review. Most often these are claims such as ineffective assistance of counsel, which require the court to consider new evidence outside the original trial record, something courts may not do in an ordinary appeal. State collateral review, though an important step in that it helps to define the scope of subsequent review through federal habeas corpus, is rarely successful. Only around 6% of death sentences are overturned on state collateral review.

(iii) Federal Habeas Corpus[12]

After a death sentence is affirmed in state collateral review, the prisoner may file for federal habeas corpus, which is a unique type of lawsuit that can be brought in federal courts. Federal habeas corpus is a species of collateral review, and it is the only way that state prisoners may attack a death sentence in a federal court (other than petitions for certiorari to the

United States Supreme Court after both direct review and state collateral review). The scope of federal habeas corpus is governed by the Antiterrorism and Effective Death Penalty Act of 1996, which restricted significantly its previous scope. The purpose of federal habeas corpus is to ensure that state courts, through the process of direct review and state collateral review, have done at least a reasonable job in protecting the prisoner's federal constitutional rights. Prisoners may also use federal habeas corpus suits to bring forth new evidence that they are innocent of the crime, though to be a valid defence at this late stage in the process, evidence of innocence must be truly compelling.

Review through federal habeas corpus is narrow in theory, but important in practice. According to Professor Eric Freedman, 21% of death penalty cases are reversed through federal habeas corpus.

James Lieberman, a professor of law at Columbia Law School, stated in 1996 that his study found that when habeas corpus petitions in death penalty cases were traced from conviction to completion of the case there was "a 40 per cent success rate in all capital cases from 1978 to 1995". Similarly, a study by Ronald Tabek in a law review article puts the success rate in habeas corpus cases involving death row inmates even higher, finding that between "1976 and 1991, approximately 47% of the habeas petitions filed by death row inmates were granted". The different numbers are largely definitional, rather than substantive. Freedman's statistics look at the percentage of all death penalty cases reversed, while the others look only at cases not reversed prior to habeas corpus review.

A similar process is available for prisoners sentenced to death by the judgement of a federal court.

(iv) Section 1983 Contested[13]

Under the Antiterrorism and Effective Death Penalty Act, a state prisoner is ordinarily only allowed one suit for habeas corpus in federal court. If the federal courts refuse to issue a writ of habeas corpus, an execution date may be set. In recent times, however, prisoners have managed to get the execution postponed through a final round of federal litigation using the Civil Rights Act of 1981 — codified at 42 U.S.C. Section 1983 — which allows people to bring law suits against state actors to protect their federal constitutional and statutory rights.

Traditionally, Section 1983 was of limited use for a state prisoner under sentence of death because the Supreme Court has held that habeas corpus, not Section 1983, is the only vehicle by which a state prisoner can challenge his judgement of death. In the 2006 *Hill* vs. *McDonough* case, however, the United States Supreme Court approved the use of Section 1983 as a vehicle for challenging a state's method of execution as cruel and unusual in violation of the Eighth Amendment. The theory is that a prisoner bringing such a challenge is not attacking directly his judgement of death, but rather the means by which that the judgement will be carried out. Therefore, the Supreme Court held in the *Hill's* case that a prisoner can use Section 1983 rather than habeas corpus to bring the law suit. Yet, as Clarence Hill's own case shows, lower federal courts have often refused to hear suits challenging methods of execution on the ground that the prisoner brought the claim too late and only for the purposes of delay. Further, the court's decision in *Baze* vs. *Rees*, upholding a lethal-injection method used by many States, has drastically narrowed the opportunity for relief through section 1983.

(V) Important Recent Cases

Before discussing some recent leading judgements of the Supreme Court of US it may be mentioned that the number of judges of the court has remained nine throughout, all 9 judges hear every case unlike in India where it has increased from 8 to 30 at present. As a result, there are no fragmented and often contradictory judgements as in India depending on which bench hears the case, even in a matter of death penalty as will be seen in Chapter 6. It may also be noted that unlike India, the US has different criminal laws for each state with different punishments for offences and each state has its own Supreme Court. Furthermore, the US Supreme Court has jurisdiction to cursorily quash a judgement of the State Supreme Court if it is in violation of the Constitution of the US, whereas the Indian Constitution gives vast jurisdiction to the Supreme Court to deal with all sorts of appeals from the High Courts, Tribunals and writ petitions.

(a) *Furman* v. *Georgia* 408 US 238 (1972)[14]
Decided on June 29, 1972 by majority of 5:4

This is one of the most important cases as it resulted in a *de facto moratorium* on death penalty in US because of different procedures followed in the States. It came to an end when *Gregy* vs. *Georgia* was decided. The Supreme Court combined *Furman's* case, which was one of murder with shooting and burglary, with *Jackson* vs. *Georgia*; in which the accused had attempted to commit armed robbery and had committed rape, and the case of *Branch* vs. *Texas* where the accused was convicted for rape.

Finding

In a five-to-four decision, the Supreme Court struck down

the imposition of the death penalties in each case as unconstitutional. Of the five justices in the majority by the narrowest opinions, Byron White and Potter Stewart expressed generalised concerns about the inconsistent application of the death penalty across a variety of cases but did not exclude the possibility of a constitutionality of death penalty law. However, Stewart and William O. Douglas worried explicitly about racial discrimination in enforcement of the death penalty. It is important to note that Justices Thurgood Marshall and William J. Brennan, Jr. expressed the opinion that the death penalty was proscribed absolutely by the Eighth Amendment as a 'cruel and unusual' punishment. Furthermore, Justice Stewart wrote: "I simply conclude that the Eighth and Fourteenth Amendments cannot tolerate the infliction of a sentence of death under legal systems that permit this unique penalty to be so wantonly and so freakishly imposed."

Justices Byron White and William O. Douglas expressed similar concerns about the apparent arbitrariness with which death sentences were imposed under the existing laws.

Justices Brennan and Marshall concurred on the grounds that death penalty was a 'cruel and unusual punishment' proscribed by the Eighth Amendment as incompatible with the evolving standards of decency of a contemporary society.

Dissents

Chief Justice Burger and the three justices in minority namely held that capital punishment had always been regarded as appropriate under the Anglo-American legal tradition for serious crimes and that the text of the Constitution implicitly authorised United States death penalty laws because of the reference in the Fourteenth Amendment to the taking of 'life'.

After *Furman's* case in the following four years, 37

States enacted new death penalty laws aimed at overcoming the court's concerns about arbitrary imposition of the death penalty. Several statutes mandating bifurcated trials, with separate guilt-innocence and sentencing phases, and imposing standards to guide and limit the discretion of juries and judges in imposing capital sentences, were upheld in a series of Supreme Court decisions in 1976, led by *Gregg* vs. *Georgia*. Other statutes enacted in response to *Furman*, which mandated imposition of the death penalty upon conviction of a certain crime such as mandatory imposition of death penalty for murder of a police officer (*Robert* vs. *Louisiana* 1977), were struck down in subsequent cases.

(b) *Gregg* vs. *Georgia* 428 US 153[15]
Decided on July 2, 1976

Chief Justice Warren E. Burger and Eight Associate Justices

The petitions of five persons who were condemned to death by the Supreme Courts of Georgia, Florida, Texas, North Carolina and Louisiana challenged the death punishment given on the ground that it violated the Eighth Amendment. The Supreme Court, however, upheld its constitutionality; more important it examined the procedural safeguards and guidelines as suggested in Furman's case were included by the State Legislature. It held that all the five States had narrowed down the eligibility criteria for giving capital punishment, and provided for right of appeal to the State Supreme Court. However, Georgia, Florida and Texas had given discretion to the trial court whether to give death punishment or not, while North Carolina and Louisiana did not. The procedural guidelines of the former group of three States were upheld as they gave discretion to the jury, while that of the latter group of two States were invalidated. It also observed that inclusion of jury in the trial enabled the court to appreciate the evolving standards in society in giving meaning to the Eighth Amendment of the US Constitution.

The petitioner, Troy Gregg, was charged with committing armed robbery and murder. In accordance with Georgia's procedure in capital cases, the trial was in two stages, a guilt stage and a sentencing stage. The evidence at the guilt trial was established.

Background

All five cases shared the same basic procedural history. After the *Furman* decision, the States of Georgia, Florida, Texas, North Carolina and Louisiana amended their death penalty statutes to meet the *Furman* guidelines. Subsequently, the five named defendants were convicted of murder and sentenced to death in their respective States. The respective State Supreme Court upheld the death sentence. The defendants then asked the US Supreme Court to review their death sentence, asking the Court to go beyond *Furman* and declare once and for all death penalty to be a 'cruel and unusual punishment' and thus in violation of the Constitution; the Court agreed to hear the cases. The Court observed that the ratio of majority in *Furman's* case the question decided was not whether the death sentence imposed on each of the individual defendant was cruel, but rather whether the process by which those sentences were imposed was rational and objectively reviewable and not that capital punishment was a cruel and unusual punishment.

Capital Punishment and the Eighth Amendment

The defendants in each of the five cases urged the Court to go farther than it had in *Furman* by holding once and for all that capital punishment was a cruel and unusual punishment that violated the Eighth Amendment. However, the Court responded that "the most marked indication of society's endorsement of the death penalty for murder is the legislative response to *Furman*." Both Congress and 35 States had complied with the Court's dictates in *Furman* by either specifying factors to be weighed and procedures to be followed when imposing a death sentence, or dictating that the death penalty would be mandatory for specific crimes. Furthermore, a referendum in California had overturned the California Supreme Court's earlier decision (*California* vs. *Anderson*) holding that the death penalty violated the California Constitution. The fact that juries remained willing to impose the death penalty also contributed to the Court's conclusion that American society did not believe in 1976 that the death penalty was in all circumstances a cruel and unusual punishment.

The Court also found that the death penalty per se is not in conflict with the basic concept of human dignity at the core of the Eighth Amendment. The death penalty serves two principal social purposes — retribution and deterrence. "In part, capital punishment is an expression of society's moral outrage at particularly offensive conduct." But this outrage must be expressed in an orderly fashion, for America is a society of laws. Retribution is consistent with human dignity, because society believes that "certain crimes are themselves so grievous, an affront to humanity that the only adequate response may be the penalty of death." And although it is difficult to determine statistically how much crime the death penalty actually deters, the Court found that in 1976 there was "no convincing empirical evidence" supporting either the view that the death penalty is an effective deterrent to crime or the opposite view. Still, the Court could not completely discount the possibility that for certain "carefully contemplated murderers", the possible penalty of death may well enter into the cold calculus that precedes the decision to act".

Finally, the Court considered whether the death penalty is "disproportionate in relation to the crime for which it is imposed." Although death is severe and irrevocable, the Court could not say that death was always disproportionate to the crime of deliberately taking human life. "It is an extreme sanction, suitable to the most extreme of crimes."

Disapproval of Mandatory Death Sentences

Although capital punishment is not *per se* cruel and unusual, it must still be carried out in a manner consistent with the evolving standards of decency that mark the progress of a maturing society. In the Court's view, the country's history with capital punishment suggests that those evolving standards of decency could not tolerate a return to the mandatory death penalty for murder that had prevailed in medieval England.

Decision of the Court

In his concurrence in *Furman*, Justice Potter Stewart remarked that death penalty was "cruel and unusual in the same way that being struck by lightning is cruel and unusual." The Court set out two broad guidelines that legislatures must follow in order to craft a constitutional capital sentencing scheme:

> First, the scheme must provide objective criteria to direct and limit the death sentencing discretion. The

objectiveness of these criteria must, in turn, be ensured by appellate review of all death sentences.

Second, the scheme must allow the sentencer (whether judge or jury) to take into account the character and record of an individual defendant.

In this case the Court found that the capital sentencing schemes of Georgia, Florida and Texas, respectively met these criteria; whereas the sentencing schemes of North Carolina and Louisiana did not.

The proposition that the death penalty was not always a cruel and unusual punishment was afirmed as. *Furman* in case had held that "where discretion is afforded a sentencing body on a matter so grave as the determination of whether a human life should be taken or spared, that discretion must be suitably directed and limited so as to minimise the risk of wholly arbitrary and capricious action." The question the Court confronted in these five cases was whether the procedures crafted by Georgia, Florida, Texas, North Carolina and Louisiana adequately minimised that risk. In all five cases, the Court's primary focus was on the jury.

Although in most criminal cases, the judge decides and imposes the sentence, "jury sentencing has been considered desirable in capital cases in order to maintain a link between contemporary community values and the penal system — a link without which the determination of punishment could hardly reflect the evolving standards of decency that mark the progress of a maturing society." Those who drafted the Model Penal Code concluded that the now-familiar bifurcated procedure, in which the jury first considered the question of guilt without regard to punishment, and then determined whether the punishment should be death or life imprisonment, was the preferable model. This was the model that the Court approved in these cases.

(c) *Atkins* vs. *Virginia*, 536 US 304 (2002)[16]
Decided on June 20, 2002 by 6:3

In this case, the Supreme Court of the United States ruled 6-3 that executing the mentally-retarded violates the Eighth Amendment's ban on cruel and unusual punishments. In applying the principles of evolving standards of society to interpret the Eight Amendment, the Supreme Court noticed that the majority of State legislatures had banned execution of mentally retarded persons. But the court left it to the individual States to decide who were mentally retarded.

The Ruling

Accordingly, the Court had previously found that death penalty was inappropriate for the crime of rape in *Coker* vs. *Georgia* (1977), or for those convicted of felony murder who neither themselves killed, attempted to kill, or intended to kill in *Enmund* vs. *Florida* (1982). The Court found that the Eighth Amendment forbids the imposition of the death penalty in these cases because "most of the legislatures that have recently addressed the matter" have rejected the death penalty for these offenders, and the Court will generally defer to the judgements of those bodies.

The Court then described how a national consensus that the mentally retarded should not be executed had emerged. In 1986, Georgia was the first State to outlaw the execution of the mentally retarded. Congress followed two years later, and the next year Maryland enacted such law. Thus, when the Court confronted the issue in *Penry's* case in 1989, it could not say that a national consensus against executing the mentally retarded had emerged.

Over the next twelve years, nineteen more States exempted the mentally retarded from capital punishment under their laws, bringing the total number of States to twenty-one, plus the Federal Government. While there are 52 States, 19 don't allow the death penalty under any circumstance, and prohibited execution of mentally retarded making 31 a clear majority of prohibition of such death penalty. In light of the "consistency of direction of change" toward a prohibition on the execution of the mentally retarded, and the relative rarity of such executions in States that still allowed it, the Court proclaimed that a "national consensus has developed against it." The Court, however, left it to individual States to make the difficult decision regarding what determined mental retardation.

This meant that inflicting the death penalty on one mentally retarded individual was less likely to deter other mentally retarded individuals from committing crimes. As for retribution, society's interest in seeing that a criminal got his 'just deserts' meant that the death penalty must be confined to the 'most serious' of murders, not simply the average murder. The goal of retribution could not be served by imposing the death penalty on a group of people who had a significantly lesser capacity to understand why they were being executed.

Minority Justices Antonin Scalia, Clarence Thomas and Chief Justice William Rehnquist argued that in spite of the increased number of States which had outlawed execution of the mentally retarded, there was no clear national consensus, and that even if there were, there was no basis in the Eighth Amendment for using such measures of opinion to determine what is 'cruel and unusual'. Chief Justice Rehnquist also criticised placing weight on foreign laws like that of the European Union in interpreting what is a cruel and unusual punishment. Prior to this case, 35 mentally retarded inmates had been executed since 1976 for crimes they had committed.

(d) *Roper* vs. *Simmons*, 543 US 551 – Supreme Court 2005[17] Decided on March 1, 2005

Justice Kennedy alongwith five Justices held that death penalty for juveniles amounted to cruel and unusual punishment and hence violated the Constitution.

The Trial Court gave death punishment to Simmons, who was 17 years old at the time of committing a murder and became 18 at the time of trial. But the State Supreme Court of Missouri following the ratio of *Atkins'* case set aside his execution as he was a juvenile of under 18 when the crime was committed.

The Supreme Court observed: "The prohibition against 'cruel and unusual punishments', like other expansive language in the Constitution, must be interpreted according to its text, by considering history, tradition and precedent, and with due regard for its purpose and function in the constitutional design. To implement this framework, we have established the propriety and affirmed the necessity of referring to the evolving standards of decency that mark the progress of a maturing society.

The conclusion that it would offend civilised standards of decency to execute a person who was less than 18 years old at the time of his or her offence is consistent with the views that have been expressed by respected professional organisations, by other nations that share our Anglo-American heritage, and by the leading members of the Western European community.

"When we heard Penry, only two death penalty States had already prohibited the execution of the mentally retarded. When we heard *Stanford*, by contrast, 12 death penalty States had already prohibited the execution of any juvenile under 18 and 15 had prohibited the execution of any juvenile under 17.

If anything, this shows that the impropriety of executing juveniles between 16 and 18 years of age gained wide recognition earlier than the impropriety of executing the mentally retarded. In the words of the Missouri Supreme Court: 'It would be the ultimate in irony if the very fact that the inappropriateness of the death penalty for juveniles was broadly recognised sooner than it was recognised for the mentally retarded were to become a reason to continue the execution of juveniles now that the execution of the mentally retarded has been barred."

"A majority of States have rejected the imposition of the death penalty on juvenile offenders under 18, and we now hold this is required by the Eighth Amendment.

"Because the death penalty is the most severe punishment, the Eighth Amendment applies to it with special force. Capital punishment must be limited to those offenders who commit 'a narrow category of the most serious crimes' and whose extreme culpability makes them 'the most deserving of execution.'

"In case of juveniles, it is recognised, it is evident that the penological justifications for the death penalty apply to them with lesser force than to adults. We have held there are two distinct social purposes served by the death penalty: 'retribution and deterrence of capital crimes by prospective offenders'."

Justices Powell and Stevens observed, "As for retribution, we remarked in *Atkins* that [i]f the culpability of the average murderer is insufficient to justify the most extreme sanction available to the State, the lesser culpability of the mentally retarded offender surely does not merit that form of retribution...." [The same applies to juveniles] although the line of 18 years of age is subject to objections.

Majority judgement made a substantial contribution to Law. Six judges held: "Our determination that the death penalty is disproportionate punishment for offenders under 18 finds confirmation in the stark reality that the United States is the only country in the world that continues to give official sanction to the juvenile death penalty. This reality does not become controlling, for the task of interpreting the Eighth Amendment remains our responsibility. Yet at least from the time of the Court's decision in *Trop*, the Court has referred to the laws of other countries and to international authorities as instructive for its interpretation of the Eighth Amendment's prohibition of cruel and unusual punishments."

"The civilised nations of the world are in virtual unanimity that...the imposition of the death penalty for crimes committed by mentally retarded offenders is overwhelmingly disapproved...; by other nations that share our Anglo-American heritage, and by the leading members of the Western European community, and observing that "[w]e have previously recognised the relevance of the views of the international community in determining whether a punishment is cruel and unusual" observing that the doctrine of felony murder has been abolished in England and India, severely restricted in Canada and a number of other Commonwealth countries, and is unknown in continental Europe. It is not irrelevant here that out of 60 major nations in the world surveyed in 1965, only three retained the death penalty for rape where death did not ensue...."

Article 37 of the United Nations Convention on the Rights of the Child, which every country in the world has ratified save for the United States and Somalia, contains an express prohibition on capital punishment for crimes committed by juveniles under 18. United Nations Convention on the Rights of the Child came into force on November 20, 1989. No ratifying country has entered a reservation to the provision prohibiting the execution of juvenile offenders.

The petitioner does not contest that only seven countries other than the United States have executed juvenile offenders since 1990: Iran, Pakistan, Saudi Arabia, Yemen, Nigeria, the Democratic Republic of Congo and China. Since then, each of these countries has either abolished capital punishment for juveniles or made public disavowal of the practice. In sum, it is fair to say that the United States now stands alone in a world that has turned its face against the juvenile death penalty.

Though the international covenants prohibiting the juvenile death penalty are of more recent date, it is instructive to note that the United Kingdom abolished the juvenile death penalty in 1930, i.e., before these covenants came into being. The United Kingdom's experience bears particular relevance here in light of the historic ties between our countries and in light of the Eighth Amendment's own origins. As of now, the United Kingdom has abolished the death penalty in its entirety....

It is proper that we acknowledge the overwhelming weight of international opinion against the juvenile death penalty, resting in large part on the understanding that the instability and emotional imbalance of young people may often be a factor in the crime. The opinion of the world community, while not controlling our outcome, does provide respected and significant confirmation for our own conclusions."

Thus, the US Supreme Court by 6 to 3 held:

> "The Eighth and Fourteenth Amendments forbid imposition of the death penalty on offenders who were under the age of 18 when their crimes were committed. The judgement of the Missouri Supreme Court setting

aside the sentence of death imposed upon Christopher Simmons is affirmed."

Prior to these cases, 22 inmates were executed after Furmani can 1976 for crimes committed while they were under the age of 18.

□

6

Death Penalty in India and Modes of Execution of Death Sentence

(a) Historical Background

As in other parts of the world, death penalty always existed in India and various diabolical methods of ending life were employed in the past. The first known person to be executed in Emperor Chandragupta Maurya's times in about 2nd century BC was Malayketu. He was one of the Army Chiefs of King Nanda of Magadh (now Bihar). He had spied for Chandragupta during the war which resulted in the defeat of King Nanda and establishment of the Maurya dynasty. For Malayketu's treachery, his hands were tied with a rope to the hoofs of a horse and he was dragged to death by King Nanda. Chandragupta Maurya's grandson, Emperor Ashoka the Great, adopted Buddhism and under Buddhist influence the modes of punishment including death punishment, were humanised but this was for a short period of Indian history.

During the Muslim and Moghul rule of India, death punishment on the vanquished was inflicted with utmost cruelty by the orders of the victorious kings who combined judicial as well as absolute political authority. Mohammad Ghazni, after defeating the Rajput King Prithviraj Chauhan, who had earlier defeated and pardoned him several times, was tortured and blinded before he was executed. For a short period in Moghul times, during the rule of Akbar and Jehangir, judicial authority was established, but the methods of death punishment often involved cruelty like throwing the condemned man down a cliff, beheading in public, crushing under an elephant's feet and so on. The cruelest period was during the reign of Aurangzeb. He not only killed his brothers to ensure his accession to the Moghul throne but imprisoned his father Shahjahan till his death to consolidate his hold on the empire. The Sikhs who waged relentless war against him were dealt with mercilessly. A Sikh Guru Banda Bairagi was sawed to death in Chandni Chowk in Delhi where Sisganj Gurudwara now stands. Similarly, two young sons of Guru Gobind Singh were buried alive by building a wall around them. Shivaji too carried on a relentless war and founded the Maratha Empire, which ultimately succeeded in defeating Aurangzeb. Shivaji had separated the judiciary but the modes of putting a criminal to death were still somewhat cruel. His son, Sambhaji, who succeeded Shivaji was arrested and killed by Aurangzeb after gruesome torture of quartering and blinding him in public at Aurangabad in Maharashtra.

The British, who first came to trade and founded the East India Company, ultimately succeeded in dominating India. During the Company Rule, as it is called, they established an administrative mechanism with the semblance of an independent judiciary. During that period, death punishment for murder and treason was the rule and sometimes the accused were given punishment of transportation for life and sent to Andamans, known as *Kala Pani*. However, the defeated kings were often transferred for life to faraway corners of India. For instance, the Burmese King Thimbwa, after the conquest of

Burma (now known as Myanmar), was sent to the western coastal town of Ratnagiri in Maharashtra, while Bahadur Shah Zafar, the last Moghul King after the Mutiny of 1857, called the first war of Independence by India, was imprisoned in Mandalay in Myanmar where he died. During this period, brutal killing of defeated generals was not uncommon. Tatya Tope, a General of the Rani of Jhansi, who fought valiantly against the British, was publicly executed by tying him to a cannon and firing it.

After 1857, India came under the direct rule of the British Crown. The Indian Penal Code was enacted in 1862 while the criminal procedure was codified in 1898. Both these laws still exist because of Article 372 of the Constitution of India which states that "all the laws in force in the territory of India immediately before the commencement of this Constitution shall continue in force therein until altered or repealed by the competent legislature or declared ultravires of the Fundamental Rights of the Constitution. Though in 1973, the old Criminal Procedure Code was repealed and a new code was enacted, it is basically the same. During the British colonial days, those who revolted against British rule were hanged, like the Ranade Brothers of Maharashtra, Khudi Ram Bose of Bengal, Chandrashekhar Azad of the United Provinces, and Bhagat Singh, Sukhdev and Rajguru from the Punjab. Revolutionaries like Vasudev Balwant Phadke and Veer Vinayak Damodar Savarkar were given transportation for life and sent to Aden and Andamans, respectively. Also the Code provided for death punishment or transportation for life for murder. The latter has now been deleted and substituted by life imprisonment. Besides, during British rule, though few Indians were included in the judiciary, they were not allowed to conduct criminal trials against any European.

(b) Penal Laws of India

Section 302 of Indian Penal Code of 1860:

"Punishment for murder: Whoever commits murder shall be punished with death or imprisonment for life, [earlier it was transportation for life which has been deleted] and also shall be liable for fine."

Section 303 — Punishment for murder by life convict

"Whoever, being under sentence of imprisonment for life, commits murder, shall be punished with death."

It is necessary to mention here that the Supreme Court of India in 1983 in the case of *Mithu* vs. *State of Punjab*,[1] struck down this Section because it did not give any discretion to the Judge as regards imposing death punishment inspite of mitigating circumstances, as was done by the US Supreme Court in *Furman's* case in 1972 as seen earlier.

The Indian Penal Code also provides for death punishment or life imprisonment for a person who abates a child under 18 years of age or an insane person to commit suicide, as a result of which he commits suicide; and under Section 396, death punishment or life imprisonment is provided for *dacoity* (armed robbery) accompanied by murder. Under Section 121, whoever wages or attempts to wage war or abets in waging war against the Government of India, shall be punished with death or imprisonment for life and shall also be liable to fine. Similarly, under Section 132, "Whoever abets the committing of mutiny by members of the Armed Forces, and if mutiny is committed in consequence of that abetment, he shall be punished with death or with imprisonment for life or other imprisonment which may extend to ten years, and shall also be liable to fine."

Criminal Procedure Code

There existed separate provincial criminal procedures since

1856, but subsequently a uniform Criminal Procedure Code was codified titled the Criminal Procedure Code of 1898 and it was replaced by the Code of 1973. Under all the procedures, death punishment was by hanging by rope.

Under Section 367 of the old Criminal Procedure Code of 1898, whenever an offence was committed for which the convict was liable to be punished with death or life imprisonment, death punishment was a rule and special reasons had to be given for giving life imprisonment. But under Section 354 of the Code of 1973, the position was reversed indicating that death punishment should be given under unusual circumstances, and not as a matter of course. Besides, reasons had to be given for imposing death punishment. Due to increasing narcotic crimes, Section 31A was inserted in 1989 to the Narcotic, Drug and Psychopathic Substance Act of 1983.

The Indian Penal Code does not bar giving death punishment to the juvenile, the mentally retarded or pregnant women as did the English law when that country had death punishment. The Indian Supreme Court has not invalidated death punishment for the first two categories of persons while a pregnant woman can be executed after delivery.

It may also be noted that in India there are very few crimes for which death punishment is given. It is not given to a person who commits rape as was the case in some States in the United States until the US Supreme Court struck down death sentence for rape unless it was accompanied with murder so as to amount to aggravated murder. Furthermore, like in America, there is less and less tendency amongst the judiciary to award death punishment in India.

But military law in India, as in other countries which have or have not abolished death sentence, is a different matter. These countries uphold death punishment when the offence threatens the security of the country or endangers the military capability of the country. In India, there are several offences which are punishable under the military law and are dealt with subsequently. Similarly, in times of war, the Law of War operates regarding persons like spies of the enemy country in civilian clothes and can be shot dead without trial.

The validity of the death punishment under Section 302 of the Indian Penal Code was squarely challenged in 1980 vide *Bachan Singh* vs. *State of Punjab*[2] before the Constitution Bench of five Judges of the Supreme Court. By a majority of 4:1, with Justice P.N. Bhagwati dissenting, the court held that death punishment is valid, is not inhumane and not violative of Articles 21 and 14 of the Constitution of India. Justice R.S. Sarkaria, speaking for the majority, appreciated the change in language of Section 354(3) that in case of murder if death punishment is to be given instead of life, special reasons should be recorded, which was a reversal of the earlier position that death punishment was the norm and special reasons had to be given for commuting it to life imprisonment. The majority held that death punishment should be given "in the rarest of rare cases, when the alternative option is unquestionably foreclosed" and when the act of murder shocks the collective conscience of the society.

Referring to the principle of "the rarest of the rare case", Justice M.P. Thakkar of three-judge Bench of the Supreme Court, in *Machi Singh's* case said that the following questions may be posed and answered:

(a) Is there something uncommon about the crime which renders sentence of imprisonment for life inadequate and calls for a death sentence.

(b) Are the circumstances of the crime such that there is no alternative but to impose death sentence even after according maximum weightage to the mitigating circumstances which speak in favour of the offender?

This Bench gave the guidelines for imposition of death sentence. These are:

(i) The extreme penalty of death need not be inflicted except in the gravest cases of extreme culpability.

(ii) Before opting for the death penalty, the circumstances of the 'offender' also require to be taken into consideration along with the circumstances of the crime.

(iii) Life imprisonment is the rule and death sentence is an exception. Death sentence must be imposed only when life imprisonment appears to be an altogether inadequate punishment having regard to the relevant circumstances of the crime, and provided, and only provided, the option to impose sentence of imprisonment for life cannot be conscientiously exercised having regard to the nature and circumstances of the crime and all the relevant circumstances.

(iv) A balance sheet of aggravating and mitigating circumstances has to be drawn up and in doing so, the mitigating circumstances have to be accorded full weightage and a just balance has to be struck between the aggravating and the mitigating circumstances before the option is exercised.[3]

In *Deena's* case,[4] Chief Justice Y.V. Chandrachud, who also presided over the Bench, however, observed that *Machi Singh's* case gave guidelines to elaborate what is meant by a rarest of the rare case? Yet "such categorisation is in the very nature of things difficult to define and even describe.... Though not to crystallise, the area of those rarest of the rare cases in which death sentence can justifiably be imposed".

To avoid arbitrariness, randomness and inconsistencies in giving death punishment or life imprisonment, it has been suggested that the legislature should give guidelines and secondly make death sentence for certain offences mandatory. But both the US Supreme Court in *Furman* vs. *Georgia* case in 1972 and later the Indian Supreme Court in 1983 in *Mithu's* case as mentioned above, have invalidated laws which did not give discretion to the Judge in the matter of awarding death punishment. Chief Justice Chandrachud observed that not to give discretion to the Judge and impose death penalty was a "relic of history". He cited several mitigating factors like a lifer on parole committing a murder on finding his wife in a compromising position or committing a murder in an act of self-defence. To deny a Judge discretion in such grave matter was not in "conformity with modern law." Justice O. Chennappa Reddy said, "Not to give discretion to a Judge and make death penalty mandatory is anarchism. Death penalty is so final, so irrevocable, and so *irreversible* that the law which provides it without involvement of judicial mind is stigmatised as arbitrary and anarchic." Similarly, Justice Byer earlier in *Furman's* case very correctly doubted if such guidelines can be given and expressed his misgivings about inflicting mandatory death punishment for certain offences.

The only solution to this complex issue seems to be that the Right of Appeal should be given to the highest court of the land, and the discretion whether a person should live or be killed should be decided by the Full Court or at least five judges and Justice P.N. Bhagwati pointed out in his celebrated dissenting judgement in *Bachan Singh's* case, where the constitutional validity of death punishment was challenged, that it should be decided by unanimous verdict and not by majority.

(c) Deena's Case[5]

In *Deena's* case, the only question challenged was the constitutional validity of executing death punishment by hanging by rope till the person is dead as provided by Criminal Procedure Code for over 150 years particularly now under Section 354(5) of the Code of Criminal Procedure. It was challenged on the ground that this was an obsolete and degrading method of executing death punishment.

The test laid down in *Deena's* case provides that the execution of death punishment should satisfy the three-fold test: (1) It should be quick and simple as far as possible and free from anything that necessarily sharpens the poignancy of the prisoner's apprehension; (2) The act of the execution should produce immediate unconsciousness of the person passing quickly into the death; and (3) It should not involve mutilation.

In *Deena's* case, the Supreme Court held that hanging by rope till the convict is dead is provided by over a century year old method prescribed by the Criminal Procedure Code was valid. Chief Justice Y.V. Chandrachud relied on Anglo-American jurisprudence on death punishment and stated that granting that the sentence of death is constitutionally valid, not even the sophisticated sensitivities can justly demand that those upon whom the extreme penalty of law is imposed because of the magnitude of their crime, should not be made to suffer the execution of that sentence, unaccompanied by torture or degradation of any kind. If the larger interests of the community as opposed to the interests of an individual require that the death sentence should be imposed in an exceptional class of cases, the same societal interests would justify the execution of that sentence, though in strict conformity with the requirements of Article 21. In this case, Chief Justice Chandrachud observed:

Though Article 21 was the focal point of this case, almost everyone of the learned counsel appearing on behalf of the petitioners drew inspiration from the Eighth Amendment to the United States Constitution which provides that "Excessive bail shall not be required, nor excessive fines imposed, nor cruel and unusual punishments inflicted."

The prohibition against cruel and unusual punishments dates back to the *Magna Carta*, though it found recognition in the English Law by its adoption in the English Declaration of Rights in 1689. The purpose of this enactment was to check the barbarous punishments which were common during the regime of the Stuarts, like pillory, disemboweling, decapitation and drawing and quartering. As a result of the English reform movement which was started in the seventeenth century by the European humanists, these punishments gradually fell into disrepute. The fundamental principle underlying the prohibition against cruel and unusual punishments was incorporated into the Bill of Rights in 1791 by the USA.

The early development of law in America shows that the prohibition against cruel and unusual punishments concerned itself with unusual cruelty only, the emphasis being on "unnecessary cruelty and pain". In *Kemmler*, death by electrocution was held not necessarily cruel. In *O' Neil* vs. *Vermont*, Justice Field, in his dissenting opinion, enlarged the concept of unusual punishment to cover penalties "which shook the sense of justice". In *Trop* vs. *Dullles*, a sharply divided Court held that divesture of citizenship was constitutionally forbidden. Chief Justice Earl Warren, speaking for three Justices, observed that the content of the Eighth Amendment was not static and that it "must draw its meaning from the evolving standards of decency that mark the progress of a maturing society". According to the learned Chief Justice, the Eighth Amendment whose "basic concept is nothing less than the dignity of man", ensures "the principle of civilised treatment". After the decision in *Trop*, the American Supreme Court has formulated a sophisticated definition of the Eighth Amendment clause in a series of important cases called the '18 Kay Cases'. A resumé of those cases can be found in *Substantive Criminal Law* by Prof. M. Cherif Bassiouni (Ed. 1978, pp. 44-45). It shows that even a second electrocution after the failure of the first attempt, provided it is not an intentional effort to inflict unnecessary suffering, was held not violative of the Eighth Amendment. It was observed in that case that....

"The cruelty against which the Constitution protects a convicted man is cruelty inherent in the method of punishment, not the necessary suffering involved in any method employed to extinguish life humanely. No one can deny that some suffering and anguish is bound to result to the condemned man at the time of execution of his death sentence. But it is not wholly inappropriate to observe that having had the opportunity to avoid that suffering and anguish, he chose the path of risking it in favour of earning some other benefit. His minimal suffering is real, but so we believe was the suffering of his victims and even so will be the suffering of the victims of those other criminals who believe that they can commit crimes of great atrocity with relative impunity."

It is this 'relative impunity' which attracts the rule in *Bachan Singh.*

Though the Eighth Amendment has thus a dynamic content which has evolved over the years as public moral perceptions changed from time to time, several concurring opinions show that in America capital punishment is not considered to be violative of the Eighth Amendment. In the words of Chief Justice Warren, "The death penalty has been employed throughout our history, and, in a day when it is still widely accepted, it cannot be said to violate the constitutional concept of cruelty." What the Eighth Amendment prohibits is "something inhuman and barbarous and something more than the mere extinguishment of life. The suffering necessarily involved in the execution of death sentence is not banned by the Eighth Amendment, though the cruel form of execution is." Therefore, according to Chief Justice Chandrachud, no sustenance can, therefore, be derived from the Eighth Amendment to the argument that either the death sentence or the method of executing that sentence by hanging is violative of Article 21 on the ground that death sentence is barbarous or that the method of hanging is cruel, inhuman or degrading. Hanging as a mode of execution is not relentless in its severity. As judges, we ought not to assume that we are endowed with a divine insight into the needs of a society. On the contrary, we should heed the warning given by Justice Frankfurter: "As history amply proves, the judiciary is prone to misconceive the public good by confounding private notions with constitutional requirements.... For these reasons, the challenge to the constitutionality of Section 354(5) of the Code of Criminal Procedure fails and the writ petitions are dismissed...."

Deena was the first to challenge the constitutional validity of hanging and because of the stay granted by Chief Justice Chandrachud several condemned persons had also challenged the method of executing death punishment, and also got the stay, as mentioned in the introduction. Deena had also challenged his death punishment as discriminatory and his case was listed to be heard only four days later on September 27, 1983, and was dismissed on merits.

With great respect, Chief Justice Chandrachud should have also given due weightage to the improving methods of extinguishing life as developed in America, trends in other parts of the world and the UN resolution given earlier.

It may be mentioned again that in *Deena's* case, the issue was confined to the method of extinguishing life by hanging when the death punishment was awarded. Attorney General K. Parasaran, appearing for the government, raised the preliminary objection that this question was also concluded in *Bachan Singh's* case. The Chief Justice overruled the preliminary objection and pointed out that though this question was addressed by the court in that case the validity of hanging as the method of imposing death punishment was not "raised squarely…nor considered directly and substantially" with the observation that the question raised in *Deena's* case:

> …is important not only from the legal and constitutional points of view but also from the sociological point of view. It will not be proper to sidetrack that question and refuse to examine it fully because of the incidental consideration which it received in *Bachan Singh*.

During the arguments in *Deena's* case, it was emphasised that the very fact that several countries had given up hanging and replaced it by other methods, such as electric chair, lethal injection or shooting, was evident of the fact that hanging to death was archaic. Several examples including Justice Bhagwati's dissenting judgement, are discussed subsequently. It may also be stated that when it was pointed out to the court that the accused of the German high command, after the Nuremberg trial gave them death punishment, wanted death by shooting instead of hanging, Justice R.S. Pathak stated that it was because they wanted military death. To that the author replied that this itself proved that hanging was a degrading method. The Supreme Court upheld the validity of hanging by rope. It also justified that the Court could not legislate and if the present method was declared unconstitutional, no death punishment could be carried out although it was held valid by a larger Constitution bench. This reasoning for upholding hanging is untenable, because if court found a law unconstitutional it has to be struck down regardless of consequences. The Supreme Court of the State of Nebraska in 2004 did invalidate the law imposing death punishment by electrocution notwithstanding the fact that there was no other law to impose death punishment. As a result, there was no death punishment in that State till the State of Nebraska passed a law for imposing death punishment by lethal injection in 2011.

The Supreme Court of India in view of earlier Reports of the Royal Commission and the Law Commission of India should have at least directed that the government should consider amending Section 354 (5) of the Criminal Procedure Code which provided for hanging in view of technological advances made in extinguishing life.

This judgement was widely reported and Congress MP and former Union Minister, Mr. Kamal Nath, had asked a question in Parliament whether the government was considering alternative methods of death punishment, to which the government replied in the negative.

The execution of the death sentence by hanging by rope has to be judged with reference to the objective factors such as international norms and international opinion, modern penological theories, development of technologies and evolving standards of human decency.

The standard of human decency with reference to death punishment is required to be judged with reference to various aspects which vary from society to society depending on its cultural and spiritual tradition, its history and philosophy and its sense of moral and ethical values. To take an example, if a sentence of cutting off the arm for the offence of theft or a sentence of stoning to death for the offence of adultery were prescribed by law, as practised in Saudi Arabia, there can be no doubt that such punishment would be condemned as barbaric and cruel in India, even though such law may be regarded as proportionate to the offence and, hence, reasonable and just in some other countries. So also the standards of human decency vary from time to time even within the same society.

It is relevant to mention that it was specifically contended that in *Maneka Gandhi's* case, the Supreme Court had held, and correctly so, that the procedure established by law to deprive a person of his life and liberty under Article 21 had to be "fair, just and reasonable". Therefore, it was logical for the Supreme Court to further expand the scope of Article 21 to hold that such a law should also be just, fair and reasonable. Unfortunately, the Supreme Court did not enlarge the scope of Article 21 in this respect.

In an evolutionary society, the standards of human decency are progressively evolving to higher levels and what was regarded as legitimate and reasonable punishment proportionate to the offence at one time, may now according to the evolving standards of human decency, be regarded as barbaric and inhuman punishment wholly disproportionate to the offence. It may be observed that even when a dog is to be killed, shooting it is no longer the norm but it is killed by giving an intravenous injection. Therefore, the question arises as to why a man should be executed through an archaic method of extinguishing life, and that too by judicial order?

In light of the above safeguards and views, it is important to note here that the view taken by Justice Bhagwati (in his dissenting judgement) in *Bachan Singh's* case[6] needs to be studied. The said view is as follows:

> "The physical pain and suffering which the execution of the sentence of death involves is also no less cruel and inhuman. In India, the method of execution followed is hanging by the rope. Electrocution or application of lethal gas has not yet taken its place as in some of the Western countries. It is, therefore, with reference to execution by hanging that I must consider whether the sentence of death is barbaric and inhuman as entailing physical pain and agony. It is no doubt true that the Royal Commission on Capital Punishment 1949-53 found that hanging is the most humane method of execution and so also in *Ichikawa* vs. *Japan* (*Vide* David Pannick on *Judicial Review of Death Penalty*, p. 73), the Japanese Supreme Court held that execution by hanging does not correspond to 'cruel punishment' inhibited by Article 36 of the Japanese Constitution. But whether amongst all the methods of execution, hanging is the most humane or in view of the Japanese Supreme Court, hanging is not cruel punishment within the meaning of Article 36, one thing is clear that hanging is undoubtedly accompanied by intense physical torture and pain. Warden Duffy of San Quentin, a high security prison in the United States of America, describes the hanging process with brutal frankness in lurid details: The day before an execution, the prisoner goes through a harrowing experience of being weighed, measured for length of drop to assure breaking of the neck, the size of the neck, body measurements etc. When the trap springs he dangles at the end of the rope. There are times when the neck has not been broken and the prisoner strangles to death. His eyes pop almost out of his head, his tongue

swells and protrudes from his mouth, his neck may be broken, and the rope many times takes large portions of skin and flesh from the side of the face that the noose is on. He urinates, he defecates, and droppings fall to the floor while witnesses look on, and at almost all executions one or more faint or have to be helped out of the witness-room. The prisoner remains dangling from the end of the rope from 8 to 14 minutes before the doctor, who has climbed up a small ladder and listens to his heartbeat with a stethoscope, pronounces him dead. A prison guard stands at the feet of the hanged person and holds the body steady, because during the first few minutes, there is usually considerable struggling in an effort to breathe. If the drop is too short, there will be a slow and agonizing death by strangulation. On the other hand, if the drop is too long, the head will be torn off. In England, centuries of practice have produced a detailed chart relating a man's weight and physical condition to the proper length of drop, but even there mistakes have been made. In 1927, a surgeon who witnessed a double execution wrote: The bodies were cut down after fifteen minutes and placed in an antechamber, when I was horrified to hear one of the supposed corpses give a gasp and find him making respiratory efforts, evidently a prelude to revival. The two bodies were quickly suspended again for a quarter of an hour longer.... Dislocation of the neck is the ideal aimed at, but, out of all my post-mortem findings that has proved rather an exception, which, in the majority of instances, the cause of death was strangulation and asphyxia."

"These passages clearly establish beyond doubt that the execution of sentence of death by hanging does involve intense physical pain and suffering, though it may be regarded by some as more humane than electrocution or application of lethal gas."

These observations of Justice Bhagwati are clear in light of the fact that most of the developed as well as developing countries have replaced hanging as the mode of execution by intravenous lethal injection or shooting. The descriptions of these methods of executions prove that death by hanging involves immense pain and suffering. It is with these views and the observations made in relation to the various other modes of execution that lethal injection becomes acceptable as the most humane method of execution of the death sentence. This mode involves less pain and suffering to the convict undergoing the death sentence. Death as a result of the hanging in most of the cases is because of asphyxia or strangulation which causes lingering and painful death of the condemned person. We may here again quote from Justice Bhagwati's judgement which is telling:

> "If this be the true mental and physical effect of death sentence on the condemned prisoner and if it causes such mental anguish, psychological strain and physical agony and suffering, it is difficult to see how it can be regarded as anything but cruel and inhuman. The only answer which can be given for justifying this infliction of mental and physical pain and suffering is that the condemned prisoner having killed a human being does not merit any sympathy and must suffer this punishment because he 'deserves' it. No mercy can be shown to one who did not show any mercy to others. But, as I shall presently point out, this justificatory reason cannot commend itself to any civilised society because it is based on the theory of retribution or retaliation and at the bottom of it lies the desire of the society to

avenge itself against the wrong-doer. That is not a permissible penological goal."

It is important to state here that the views expressed by Justice Bhagwati in the above-mentioned case are not a result of any bias as is clear because he states, "I may make it clear that the question to which I am addressing myself is only in regard to the proportionality of death sentence to the offence of murder...."

It is important to note that Justice Bhagwati confines his opinion as regards murder only and specifically excludes imposition of inflicting capital punishment for the offence of "treason or any other offences involving the security of the State."

It is also relevant to mention here the viewpoint adopted by the Supreme Court in *Deena's* case with regard to lethal injection based on the information and practice of its use prevalent more than two decades ago. It was observed:

> "What remains now to consider is the system of lethal injection. The Royal Commission has discussed that method in paragraphs 735 to 749 of its Report. Lethal injection is by and large an untried method. But that is not its most serious defect. The injection is required to be administered intravenously, which is a delicate and skilled operation. The Prison Medical Officers, who were interviewed by the Royal Commission, doubted whether the system of lethal injection was more humane than hanging (see paragraph 739 of the Report). The British Medical Association told the Commission that no medical practitioner should be asked to take part in bringing about the death of a convicted murderer and that the Association would be most strongly opposed to any proposal to introduce a method of execution which would require the

services of a medical practitioner, either in carrying out the actual process of killing or in instructing others in the technique of that process. The Commission expressed its conclusions in paragraph 749 by saying that it could not recommend that, in the present circumstances, lethal injection should be substituted for hanging since they were not satisfied that executions carried out by the administration of lethal injections would bring about death more quickly, painlessly and decently in all cases. The Commission, however, recommended, unanimously and emphatically, that the question should be periodically examined, especially in the light of the progress made in the science of anesthetics."[7]

This was also, as mentioned earlier, the opinion of the Law Commission of India expressed in its 35th Report of 1967. In upholding the death punishment by hanging, the Supreme Court relied on the conditions that existed over a quarter century ago.

It may be mentioned here that in *Deena's* case, the Supreme Court upheld the constitutional validity of Section 354(5) of Code of Criminal Procedure of 1973 for carrying out death sentence by hanging by neck till the convict is dead as the best available method as compared to electric chair, shooting or lethal injection, without examining other methods of extinguishing life practised in the world. The process of hanging starts a day earlier as the condemned person is weighed. Furthermore, his legs are tied, hands are held by the guards, and the black mask is put on his head before he is hanged. This causes further punishment, although the judgement holds that no further agony should be caused. It may be noted that the hands and legs are restrained and the mask is kept not for the benefit of the condemned person but for the benefit of people who are present for carrying out the death punishment by hanging as they cannot bear the last sight of restlessness of the condemned person. Furthermore, because many times, the tongue and eyes protrude, a black mask is placed on the convict's head. As the person is kept hanging till death and as there is no provision for postmortem, it is not known whether death was caused by painful strangulation or instantaneously by breaking of the spinal cord.

It may also be mentioned that the Supreme Court observed that the method of shooting to death was practised in dictatorships. But this is not fully correct. In fact, the Army, Navy and Air Force Acts in India give discretion to the Court Martial tribunal to hold that the condemned person be hanged to death or be shot to death, as mentioned earlier. It may be further noticed that hanging has been given up in several States in the United States of America and substituted by electrocution or lethal injection. In thirty-four States, execution is carried by lethal injection. These methods are adopted as they are more civilized and hanging has been abolished by most of these states in the USA. However, even the Constitutional validity of lethal injection is now being examined by the Supreme Court of United States on the ground that it violates the Eighth Amendment of the US Constitution which prohibits cruel and unusual punishment and it may in the near future examine the question of execution by electrocution as unconstitutional. Surprisingly, so far the question of method of hanging has not been challenged in the US Supreme Court.

In India, in case of Central Jails there are no facilities for administering intravenous lethal injection. In such cases, vehicles with all the required equipments and competent persons to administer the lethal injection to the convict can be sent. It is equally important to note that in present times, there is scarcity of competent hangmen in the country and there are cases where persons are not executed for want of such hangmen. Furthermore, the Jail Manual speaks of training inexperienced hangmen to acquire expertise. Often inexperience persons are employed and use of inexperienced persons increases the chances of lingering death by strangulation instead of instantaneous death by breaking of vertebra.

(d) Judicial Discretion Regarding Death Punishment in Parliament[8]

Since under Indian law, discretion is given to a judge whether to give death punishment or life imprisonment, Atal Bihari Vajpayee, former Prime Minister of India, had tabled a Constitution Amendment Bill that every person under the sentence of death should have the right to move the highest court of the land. To buttress his views, he referred to judicial adhocism and fragmented nature of the benches in the higher judiciary with in-built views of a judge in exercising this colossal discretion. He pointed out that this bias existed because of the personal psychology of a judge from the lowest to the highest court. He quoted extensively from the famous dissenting judgement of Justice P.N. Bhagwati in *Bachan Singh's* case to underscore his point. He also pointed out that in two identical gruesome bride-burning cases, one Bench of the Supreme Court gave life imprisonment in the first case while the other gave death punishment in the second. To minimise this discretion, he suggested that Parliament should frame some guidelines and right to appeal should be provided to the Supreme Court in every case of death punishment. He also pointed out that the right to appeal was given earlier in disputes involving ₹ 20,000 or more; to advocates aggrieved by decisions of the Bar Council of India or to Members of the Assembly and Parliament aggrieved by decisions of the High Court under the Representation of the

People's Act. He emphasised that right to appeal to the Supreme Court be given when death punishment was so irreversible and irrevocable, so that a person would have the satisfaction that his appeal has been heard at the highest level of the judiciary. He hoped all parties would support his amendment. It led to a long debate and speaker after speaker, regardless of party affiliation, unanimously appreciated his contribution on this all-important question of death punishment and supported his amendment. Hans Raj Bhardwaj, the then Law Minister of India, said he was not opposed to the Bill in principle. However, he felt that instead of a constitutional amendment, an amendment to enlarge the Supreme Court's jurisdiction would serve the purpose. Therefore, Vajpayee did not press for a vote and agreed to withdraw the amendment. However, so far a law to give this right to appeal to the aggrieved has not yet been enacted.

(e) Death Punishment under Military Law and the Law of War[9]

Civilians are given death punishment under the Criminal Procedure Code for murder but under military laws which include the Army and Air Force Act of 1950 and the Navy Act of 1957, death punishment is also given to a person for a number of other offences including murder.

These offences briefly are:

(a) Shamefully abandons a post which is his duty to defend or induces one to do so;

(b) Induces anyone to abstain or discourages any one from acting against the enemy;

(c) In the presence of the enemy, shamefully discards weapons and behaves in such a manner which shows cowardice;

(d) Treacherously holds correspondence, communication or intelligence from the enemy;

(e) Assists the enemy with arms, ammunition, supplies, etc.;

(f) Treacherously or by cowardice raises a flag of truce to the enemy;

(g) Causes to spread reports calculated to create alarm or disprudency during war or military operations;

(h) Leaves his post he is supposed to guard without leave in time of war;

(i) Protects or harbours enemy who is not a prisoner of war;

(j) As a prisoner of war, voluntarily aids the enemy;

(k) Being a sentry during the time of war, sleeps or is intoxicated;

(l) Acts calculated to threaten success of military operations;

(m) Commits any offence in participating, encouraging and does not suppress mutiny against military, naval and air force of India;

(n) Out of cowardice deserts his post, sleeps upon his watch when ordered to take action against the enemy;

(o) Fails when he is duty-bound to destroy the property if such act is committed with intent to assist the enemy;

(p) Withholds from or gives intelligence reports to the enemy;

(q) Gives supplies to the enemy or voluntarily serves or aids the enemy when made a prisoner of war;

(r) Incites any person to abstain against the enemy;

(s) Treacherously or shamefully causes capture or destruction of aircraft;

(t) Uses false signals or interference with any air operations;

(u) Treacherously or shamefully fails to carry out air operations;

(v) Surrenders a ship, aircraft of the navy or naval establishment to the enemy when it can be successfully defended;

(w) Is guilty of arson, or destroys naval property such as ships, ammunition and aircraft which do not belong to the enemy.

In addition, any person who is not under the military laws, who is or acts as a spy for the enemy may be given death punishment.

Court Martial

Persons who are alleged to have committed any of the above-mentioned offences are tried by General Court Martial consisting of five to nine officers. Such a Court Martial Tribunal is constituted by the Chief of Staff of the particular branch of Service. Death punishment is given by two-third and not simple majority. Earlier, judgements on an accused being guilty or not guilty could be given without giving any reasons. But after the Supreme Court judgement in *Prithi Singh Bedi's* case, the law was amended and reasons had to be given for the GCM coming to its conclusion.[10]

Furthermore, punishment is not to be carried out unless it is confirmed by the Chief of Staff and the Ministry of Defence, who confirm or commute the sentence on examination of record of the file. Earlier, there was no provision of appeal and the aggrieved person used to file a writ petition under Article 226 of the Constitution in the High Court and this used to involve a lot of delay.

In 2000, when the Law Commission of India asked for the views of members of the three armed forces regarding filing of appeals against the order a Court Martial, the heads of the Judge Advocate-General of all three services–Army, Air Force and Navy–responded that no appeal should be filed in the Supreme Court.[11] In their discussions, members of the armed forces and Judge Advocates of the three Services were of the opinion that a tribunal should be constituted to enable the aggrieved person to file an appeal. The Law Commission in its report proposed the constitution of the Armed Appellate Forces Tribunal and in 2007, the Armed Forces Tribunal Act providing for appeal was passed.[12] The tribunal under the Act consists of a three-member Bench presided over by a sitting or retired judge of the Supreme Court and two retired members of the armed forces. Appeal under the order of the, tribunal lies as of right to the Supreme Court and the jurisdiction of all other courts is barred. Thus, the final decision now rests with the highest judicial authority under the Constitution.[13]

Law Regarding Enemy Alien

It has already been mentioned that under the Army, Navy and Air Force Acts, a person who is a spy or has been caught spying or engaged in activities endangering the security and integrity and sovereignty of the country can be given death punishment even if he does not belong to the armed forces by the Court Martial. This is during peace times but in times of war, the situation is entirely different.

In the latter case, what comes into play is the International Law of War which came into existence through the Hague Declaration of 1899 and 1904 and was codified by the Geneva Convention by the League of Nations. This governs relations between countries at war and is universally recognised. Under this law, soldiers captured in uniform of an enemy state are given the status of Prisoners of War (POWs), and as such, they cannot be shot if unarmed. They also cannot be forced to fight against their own country and officers cannot be subjected to manual labour. The Red Cross is permitted to deliver mail and goods to these POWs free of duty. They also have the right to repatriation to their own country after the termination of war. But if an enemy is caught in civilian clothes, he has no right as is accorded to a POW and can be shot without any trial.

When the United Nations Charter was framed in 1945 with considerable emphasis on human rights and fundamental rights, and the Constituent Assembly debated the provisions of the Constitution of India which came into force on January 26, 1950, the framers of these documents were aware of the International Law of War. At that time international law recognised the existence of state of war with the official declaration and its termination with conclusion of a peace treaty. There was nothing in between. But in the second half of the twentieth century, this situation underweat a sea-change. There have been wars without any official declaration such as the Korean War of 1950, Sino-Indian War of 1962, Indo-Pak Wars of 1965 and 1971, the Kargil War of 1999 and the recent Iraq War. But in these undeclared wars, the Geneva Convention has been followed and its violation was declared a crime against humanity and persons responsible could be tried and punished as they were during the Nuremberg and Tokyo trials after the termination of World War II.

In this context, it is relevant to note the rights of persons under the Indian Constitution. Article 21 guarantees persons not to be deprived of right to life and liberty without the procedure established by law. Clauses (1) and (2) of Article 22 state that persons arrested under criminal law have the right to be informed of the grounds of arrest as soon as possible. Also the right to consult and be defended by a lawyer of his choice and right to be produced before a magistrate within 24 hours.

But Clause (3) of this article states that none of the rights given in clauses (1) and (2) are available to "any person (a) who for the time being is an enemy alien and (b) who is arrested or detained under any law providing for preventive detention." Clauses (4) to (7) give to the detenue some safeguards to regain his liberty such as right to be informed about the grounds of detention, right to make representation to the detaining authority and to the Advisory Board and empowers Parliament to make laws regarding the procedure for fixing time limit or constitution and procedure for the Advisory Board.[14]

But the fact is no such rights whatever are given to an enemy alien under Clause (3)(a) of Article 22. When the Constituent Assembly discussed this article on September 15, 1949, there was a long drawn debate about the likely abuse of preventive detention laws but not a whisper about an 'enemy alien'. Introducing this article, Dr. B.R. Ambedkar also said that there cannot be any controversy on this point. At that time, he said, "Exigency of individual liberty should not be placed above the interest of state or of defence services of the country." Although who is an 'enemy alien' is not defined, the words used in the Constitution that he is one "who for the time being is an enemy alien", implies that it applies to persons belonging to a country or countries who are at war with India.

In a nutshell, an 'enemy alien' is a class by itself to whom law of war applies. According to Basu, "Framing of the Constitution, the Parliament has a power to make laws regarding enemy alien provided he is detained under preventive detention law."

Now the question arises who is an enemy alien. According to 'The Halsbury's Laws of England', enemy alien is the citizen of a country which is "at war with the crown". In other words, there should be a state of war to categorise a person as 'enemy alien'.

But, and this is a great but, if an enemy alien not in uniform is arrested, he has no rights whatsoever. Such a person is treated as a spy and he can be shot dead during a war. He can also be detained without the right of habeas corpus. No human rights or fundamental liberties under the UN Charter and even our Constitutional rights are made available to him.

Non-conventional War

Now the world, particularly since the last decade of the twentieth century, is facing different types of wars which are threatening the integrity and security of countries and taking innocent lives of unarmed civilians including personnel in uniform in encounters. There are two types of terrorist wars. One is waged by those who owe allegiance to a country and are motivated by an ideology like Islam and second are those who belong to a hostile country and are armed, trained and financed by countries like Pakistan which engage in an inexpensive proxy war against India. In both cases, the attackers are not in uniform nor are they 'owned' by countries to which they belong. Such proxy wars should be treated as wars and International Laws of War should apply and those caught without should be shot dead without trial.

It is time the international community deals with such situations including those countries which shelter, train and arm terrorists to safeguard peace. Secondly, they are in a position to acquire sophisticated conventional weapons. Their acquiring nuclear weapons is also not beyond the realm of possibility. Such terrorists are not responsible to the population of any country like the governments of other countries and may even employ nuclear attack. If the world and the United Nations do not take serious cognizance of such situation, arms control and disarmament treaties or further disarmament negotiations would have no meaning.

□

7

Appeal Procedure in Cases of Death Penalty

(a) Introduction

Before examining the process of confirming death penalty in India, it is pertinent to note the Resolution of the 12th Committee of the United Nations, which reads as under:

> Every human being has an inherent right to life. This right is protected by law. No one shall be arbitrarily deprived of his life...anyone sentenced to death shall have the right to seek pardon or commutation of the sentence...sentence of death shall not be imposed for crimes committed by person below the age of 18 years and shall not be carried out on a pregnant woman.

And as has been mentioned earlier, the Resolution of the Economic and Social Council (ECOSOC) also refers to safeguard No. 6, which reads as under:

> Anyone sentenced to death shall have the right to appeal to a court of higher jurisdiction and steps should be taken to ensure that such appeals shall become mandatory.

Under the Indian Penal Code of 1860, the District Judge is empowered with the discretion to give death punishment or life imprisonment for offences of murder, conspiracy to murder abetting suicide by a minor, lunatic or person under intoxication committing suicide, waging or attempting to wage war or abetting of waging war against Government of India, aiding escape of, rescuing or harboring a prisoner of war, and abetment of mutiny committed in the consequence thereof. Earlier, a person convicted of life imprisonment committing a murder had to be given death punishment, but this provision was struck down by the Supreme Court in *Mithu's* case on the ground that no discretion was given to the court, though there could be mitigating circumstances to commit murder such as sudden provocation or finding a spouse in a compromising situation with his wife while on parole.[1]

After making analysis of the arbitrariness and inconsistencies in imposing death punishment or life imprisonment, Prof. A.R. Black Shield in his article on "Capital Punishment in India"[2] observed:

> "But where life and death sentence are given inconsistently which is understandable may not be acceptable. Mirror of criminal law is always dark and distorted."
>
> Marquis de Lafayaehe said:
>
> I shall ask for abolition of penalty of death and till the infallibility of human judgement demonstrated to me.

In the same line, former Chief Justice of India P.B. Gajendragadkar said: "A judge is yet to be born who has not committed mistakes."

Right of Appeal to the Supreme Court of India

There are many provisions in the Code of Criminal Procedure, 1973 (Cr.PC) which enable the High Court to award or confirm the death sentence. Under Section 368 of the Code, a High Court is required to confirm the death sentence passed by the Court of Session. The High Court can withdraw a case pending before a subordinate court and can try it itself and pass death sentence (Section 407, Cr.PC). The High Court, on appeal against an order of acquittal passed by a Court of Session, can convict a person and pass sentence of death [Section 386(a), Cr.PC]. Apart from this, the High Court while exercising power of enhancing the sentence can award the sentence of death [Section 386(c), Cr.PC]. But as of now, appeal to the Supreme Court cannot be filed **as of right** in all the cases where the High Court has passed the death sentence.

It is only in the following four types of cases, where the High Court passes a sentence of death, can appeal to the Supreme Court be filed **as of right**:

(i) where High Court convicts a person on a trial held by it in its extraordinary criminal jurisdiction. [Section 374(1), Cr.PC]

(ii) where High Court has withdrawn for trial before itself any case from any court subordinate to it and in such trial convicts the accused person and sentences him to death. (Art. 134(1)(b) of the Constitution of India)

(iii) Where High Court on appeal reverses an order of acquittal of an accused person and sentence him to death. [Art.134(1)(a) of the Constitution, Section 2 of the Supreme Court Enlargement of Criminal Appellate Jurisdiction] Act, 1970, and (Sec. 379 of the Cr.PC).

(iv) Right to appeal to the Supreme Court is also provided where the High Court on appeal reverses an order of acquittal of an accused person and sentences him to imprisonment for life or imprisonment for a term of 10 years or more. (Section 379 of the Cr.PC and Sec. 2 of the aforesaid Act of 1970).

However, in the following cases, a person against whom death sentence is passed or confirmed by the High Court, no appeal to the Supreme Court **as of right** is provided:

where the High Court under Section 368 of the Cr.PC confirms the sentence of death awarded by the Court of Session, no appeal as of right can be preferred to the Supreme Court.

But against an order of confirmation of death sentence passed by the High Court, there is no further right of first appeal to the Supreme Court, unless the High Court in exercise of its power under Article 134 (1)(c) grants leave to appeal to the Supreme Court, or, the Supreme Court grants special leave under Art. 136 (1) of the Constitution for an appeal being preferred.

(b) Right to Appeal to Supreme Court

It may be mentioned that the right of appeal in civil cases was guaranteed till 1979 under the pre-amended Article 133 of the Constitution when the pecuniary value of the subject matter was more than ₹ 20,000. Similarly, under the Advocates Act, 1961, right of appeal to the Supreme Court is guaranteed against the decision of the Bar Council of India under Section 38, which reads as follows:

Appeal to the Supreme Court —Any person aggrieved by an order made by the disciplinary committee of the Bar Council of India under Section 36 or Section 37 may, within sixty days of the date on which the order is communicated to him, prefer an appeal to the Supreme Court and the Supreme Court may pass such order (including an order varying the punishment awarded by the disciplinary committee of the Bar Council of India) thereon as it deems fit:

Provided that no order of the disciplinary committee of the Bar Council of India shall be varied by the Supreme Court so as to prejudicially affect the person aggrieved without giving him a reasonable opportunity of being heard.

Similarly, under the Representation of Peoples Act, 1951, the right of appeal is guaranteed under Section 116A which reads as follows:

116A. Appeals to Supreme Court – (1) Notwithstanding anything contained in any other law for the time being in force, an appeal shall lie to the Supreme Court on any question (whether of law or fact) from every order made by the High Court under Section 98 or Section 99. **(2)** Every appeal under this Chapter shall be preferred within a period of thirty days from the date of the order of the High Court under section 98 or section 99:

Provided that the Supreme Court may entertain an appeal after the expiry of the said period of thirty days if it is satisfied that the appellant had sufficient cause for not preferring the appeal within such period.

Also, under the Monopolies & Restrictive Trade Practices Act, 1969, the right to appeal to the Supreme Court is guaranteed under Section 55, which reads as follows:

Appeals – Any person aggrieved by any decision on any question referred to in clause (a), clause (b) or clause (c) of section 2A, or any other made by the Central Government under Chapter III or Chapter IV, or, as the case may be, or the Commission under Section 12A or Section 13 or section 36D or Section 37, may, within sixty days from the date of the order, prefer an appeal to the

Supreme Court on one or more of the grounds specified in Section 100 of the Code of Civil Procedure, 1908.

If the right of appeal to the Supreme Court is guaranteed in such matters, the question arises as to why appeal as of right should not be granted against death penalty imposed by the High Court, when death punishment has more serious consequences and is qualitatively different from any other punishment as it is irreversible and there is no scope for correcting an error. Further, there is observations of Justice Bhagwati in *Bachan Singh's* case[3] that in every case where the death sentence is confirmed by the High Court there shall be an automatic review of the death sentence by the Supreme Court sitting as a whole and that the death sentence shall not be affirmed or imposed by the Supreme Court unless it is approved unanimously by the entire court. It may be mentioned that the practice of the full bench hearing cases in the Supreme Court and the State Supreme Courts in the United States is an example in point.

In *E.K.Chandrasenan's* case,[4] the Supreme Court held that it can *suo-motu* enhance the punishment to death sentence.

Since there is no provision *suo-motu* to enhance the punishment to death, the author feels that the Supreme Court should not have this discretion as there can be no appeal over such irreversible punishment.

(c) Judicial Adhocism in Avoiding Death Sentence in Harbans Singh's Case[5]

A classic example of judicial adhocism and arbitrariness in imposition of death penalty is demonstrated in Supreme Court's *Harbans Singh* case. In this case, the three accused, Jeeta Singh, Kashmira Singh and Harbans Singh, were sentenced to death by the Allahabad High Court on October

20, 1975 for playing an equal part in murdering a family of four persons. Each of these three persons preferred a separate petition in the Supreme Court for special leave to appeal against the common judgement sentencing them all to death penalty. The special leave petition of Jeeta Singh came up for hearing before a Bench consisting of Justices Y.V. Chandrachud, V.R. Krishna Iyer and N.L. Untwalia, and was dismissed on April 15, 1976. Then came the special leave petition preferred by Kashmira Singh from jail. This petition was placed for hearing before another Bench consisting of Justices P.N. Bhagwati and Murtaza Fazal Ali, and leave to appeal was granted to Kashmira Singh limited to the question of sentence and by an order dated April 10, 1977 his appeal was allowed and his sentence of death was commuted to one of life imprisonment.

The result was that while Kashmira Singh's death sentence was commuted to life imprisonment by one Bench, the death sentence imposed on Jeeta Singh was confirmed by another Bench and he was executed on October 6, 1981, though both had played an equal part in the murder of the family and there was nothing to distinguish the case of one from that of the other.

The special leave petition of Harbans Singh then came up for hearing and that time it was still another Bench of Justices R.S. Sarkaria and P.N. Shinghal heard his special leave petition and rejected it on October 16, 1978. Harbans Singh (appealed) for review of this decision, but the review petition was dismissed by Justices Sarkaria and A.P. Sen on May 9, 1980. It appears that though the registry of the court had mentioned in its office report that Kashmira Singh's death sentence was already commuted, that fact was not brought to the notice of the court specifically when the special leave petition of Harbans Singh and his review petition were dismissed. Now since his special leave petition as also his review petition were dismissed, Harbans Singh would have been executed on October 6, 1981 along with Jeeta Singh, but fortunately for him he filed a writ petition in the Supreme Court and it stayed his execution. When this writ petition came up for hearing before yet another Bench consisting of Justices Chandrachud, D.A. Desai and A.N. Sen, it was pointed out that the death sentence imposed on Kashmira Singh had been commuted by a Bench consisting of Justices Bhagwati and Fazal Ali. The Bench then directed that the case be sent back to the President for reconsideration of his clemency petition. Harbans Singh's sentence was commuted to life imprisonment. As a result, Harbans Singh and Kashmira Singh escaped the gallows while Jeeta Singh was executed.

To remedy such unfortunate eventualities, the Supreme Court made the following observations:

> The fate of Jeeta has a posthumous tale to tell. He cannot profit by the direction which we propose to give because he is now beyond the process of human tribunals. But we direct that prior to the actual execution of any death sentence, the jail superintendent should ascertain personally whether the sentence of death imposed on any of the co-accused of the prisoner who is due to be hanged has been commuted. If it has been commuted, the Superintendent should apprise the superior authorities of the matter, who in turn must take prompt steps for bringing the matter to the notice of the court concerned.[5]

There is also no coherence among the judges on what should be the mitigating circumstances to convert death sentences to that of life imprisonment. For example, the young age of an accused has been considered as a mitigating factor and the Supreme Court has reduced the death sentence to life imprisonment as in cases of *Suman Dass*,[6] *Raghubir Singh*[7] and *Gurudas Singh*,[8] whereas this (young age) was not considered as a ground for reducing death sentence in cases of *Bhagwan Swaroop*[9] and *Ragho Mai*.[10]

Similarly, in some cases constructive or joint liability has been considered as a ground for giving death sentence as in cases of *Babu*,[11] *Masalti*,[12] *Gurucharan Singh*[13] and *Mukhtiar Singh*.[14] But the recent trend has been to award death punishment to the accused who gave the fatal blow or shot. However, this also has an exception, for example, in *Mrs. Indira Gandhi's assassination* case; *Kehar Singh*[15] was given death punishment on the basis of joint liability along with Satwant Singh, who actually shot her. There is also discrepancy as regards the delay in inflicting death punishment on the ground of psychological agony of the accused on being in the death row. In cases of *Ediga Anamma*,[16] *Bhoor Singh*,[17] *Gurudas Singh*[18] and *Raghubir Singh*[19], delay in executing death punishment was taken as a mitigating ground and commuted to life sentence. In fact, in *Raghubir Singh's* case, 20 months' delay was given as a ground for converting death sentence to life imprisonment, but in the case of *Bharwad Mepa*,[20] there was no commutation even though he had spent more than two years on the death now. Recently, in *Dhananjoy's* case[21] he was executed after 14 years' delay. In fact, in *Yogendra Morarji's* case, the Supreme Court observed that "we cannot obviously feed into judicial computer all such [mitigating] situations."[22]

The reasons given by the judges in a number of cases for imposing the death penalty are that the murder is 'brutal', 'cold-blooded', 'deliberate', 'unprovoked', 'fatal', 'gruesome', 'wicked', 'callous', 'heinous' or 'violent'. But the use of these labels for describing the nature of the murder is indicative only of the degree of the judges' aversion to the nature or manner of commission of the crime and it is possible that different judges may react differently to these situations. Moreover, some judges may not regard this factor as having any relevance to the imposition of death penalty and may, therefore, decline to accord to it the status of 'special reasons'. In fact, there are numerous cases, where despite the murder being one falling within these categories, the judges have refused to award death sentence. But in several other cases, death sentence was awarded. This is because of natural difference in values and social philosophy that varies from judge to judge.

In *Chandra Mohan Tiwari's* case,[23] the Supreme Court held that as per Section 377 of the Cr.PC, the State Government or the Central Government, as the case may be, may direct the public prosecutor to present an appeal to the High Court against the sentence passed by a trial court on the ground of inadequacy. The High Court may enhance the sentence to a sentence of death after giving an opportunity of hearing to the convict (Sec. 386(c)(iii), Cr.PC). The High Court can enhance the sentence passed by a trial court not only where the State has preferred an appeal against the sentence, but also where no appeal has been preferred by the State on the ground of inadequacy of sentence, in exercise of its *suo-motu* revisional power vested in it under Section 397 read with Section 401 Cr.PC.

The Supreme Court in *Nadir Khan's* case,[24] has held that the High Court while exercising its criminal revisional jurisdiction has power to act *suo-motu* to enhance the sentence in appropriate case even in the absence of an appeal against the adequacy of sentence as provided in Section 377 of the Cr.PC. Again in *Sahib Singh's* case,[25] the Supreme Court has observed that failure on the part of the State Government to prefer an appeal does not preclude the High Court from exercising *suo-motu* power of the revision under Section 397 read with Section 401 of the Cr.PC, since the High Court itself is empowered to call for the record of proceedings of any court subordinate to it. But before enhancing the sentence, the High Court has to give notice and opportunity of hearing on the question of sentence to the convict, either in person or through counsel (see also *Surjit Singh's* case).[26] It is evident that the High Court can enhance the sentence under its *suo-motu* revisional power, even without an appeal being filed by the State. But where the High Court enhances the sentence passed by trial court and even gives the death sentence, no appeal, as of right can be preferred in the Supreme Court against the order of enhancement of sentence. As discussed, in both the circumstances mentioned above, no appeal, as of right, to the Supreme Court can be preferred against the judgement of the High Court where it has awarded the death sentence. Appeal can only be filed either when a certificate under Article 134 (1)(c) of the Constitution of India has been granted by the High Court that the case is fit for appeal to the Supreme Court, or if the Supreme Court itself grants leave to appeal under Article 136(1) of the Constitution of India. But as of right no appeal can be preferred to the Supreme Court in such circumstances.

Death sentence can be passed by a Court Martial constituted under the Army Act, 1950, Air Force Act, 1950, and the Navy Act, 1957, and this has to be confirmed by the Central Government or by other authorities. But until recently there was no provision under which appeal against such an order could be filed. Earlier, even special leave to appeal to the Supreme Court against such an order of the Court Martial did not lie under Article 136(1) of the Constitution in view of the bar contained under Article 136(2) of the Constitution of India. But with the enactment of the Armed Forces Tribunal Act, 1997, this position has changed and appeal against the aforesaid Appellate Tribunal lies in the Supreme Court of India by way of Special Leave Petition.

□

8

Execution Procedure of Death Sentence in India[1]

Death sentence in India is carried out by only two modes: hanging by neck till death under criminal law and being shot to death under military laws. Every State has its own elaborate procedure for hanging in their jail manuals. Once death sentence is awarded and confirmed after exhausting all possible remedies, the execution is carried out in accordance with Section 354(5) of the Code of Criminal Procedure, 1973, i.e. hanging by neck till death. It is also provided under The Air Force Act, 1950, Army Act, 1950 and The Navy Act, 1957 that the execution has to be carried out either by hanging by neck till death or being shot to death. In India, military personal do not have the choice of selecting the method of execution, but it is decided by the Court Marshal Tribunal. If it decides that the death punishment be carried out by hanging, it is done in jail according to the procedure prescribed by the jail manual.

The jail manuals of the respective States prescribe in detail the procedure to be carried out for this mode of extinguishing life. The Jail Manual of Punjab and Haryana of 1988, which earlier was the Jail Manual of Punjab of 1890, contains the typical procedure followed in all States of India stating various steps leading to the execution of the death sentence. This procedure is contained in paragraphs 847 to 874 of Chapter XXXI of the present Jail Manual of Punjab and Haryana of 1988, which is briefly as follows.

Conditions of Confinement

Every prisoner under the sentence of the death shall, immediately on his arrival in the prison after sentence, be searched by, or by order of the Deputy Superintendent, and all articles shall be taken from him which the Deputy Superintendent deems it dangerous or inexpedient to leave in his possession. Every such prisoner is confined in a cell apart from all other prisoners, and is guarded during the day and night. After such prisoner is admitted in the jail, the Deputy Superintendent is required to examine the cell and has to satisfy himself that it is secure and has no article which can be used as a weapon or instrument with which the prisoner can commit suicide. The said Deputy Superintendent also has to ensure that there is nothing in the cell which in his opinion is inexpedient to permit its remaining in such cell. Every cell in which such convict who is under sentence of death, is at any time to be confined, shall, before such convict is placed in it, be examined by the Deputy Superintendent, or other officer appointed in that behalf, who shall satisfy himself that it is secure and contains no article of any kind which the prisoner could by any possibility use as a weapon of offence or as an instrument with which to commit suicide, or which it is, in the opinion of the Superintendent, inexpedient to permit to remain in such cell.

The Manual also describes various restrictions pertaining to the use of apparel, etc.

The convict is to be provided *Munj* mat or *Bhabbar* mat. This clause is intended to avoid presence of any substance which can be used by the prisoner as an instrument for committing suicide.

Such a prisoner is not allowed to meet or communicate with any person not authorised by the Jail Superintendent. Facilities for raising an alarm in case he tries to commit suicide are provided.

Management of Keys, Conditions under which the Door may be Opened

The keys of the cell in which a condemned prisoner is confined shall be kept by the head warden on duty who, on hearing the alarm, shall proceed to such a cell which, in case of emergency such as attempt by the prisoner to commit suicide or escape, he shall enter and with the help of the sentry frustrate such an attempt.

At no other time shall the door of the cell in which a condemned prisoner is confined, be opened without first handcuffing him and so securing him against the possibility of using violence or, if he declines to be handcuffed, unless at least three members of the establishment are present but in case of female prisoners, they are not handcuffed but are accompanied by three female wardens before the door is opened to walk in the cell yard.

The locks in use in a condemned cell shall be such as cannot be opened by any keys in use in the jail, other than those properly belonging to them.

The condemned prisoner and the cell shall be searched twice a day by the Deputy Superintendent or persons under his direction and a note of this being done and the result is to be recorded in his journal. The cell has to be lighted from sunset to sunrise.

The condemned prisoner is given the same food which is given to other convicts under rigorous imprisonment but food is not served with metal utensils like other convicts but is given in earthenware containers to check any possibility of committing suicide. Furthermore, food is given not along with other prisoners.

During the confinement, he is given books of his choice and writing material but newspapers are not allowed. If he is a smoker, cigarettes are provided. Special indulgence is given in case of interviews with relatives, friends and priests.

In case of a woman convict, daily examination of the cell or person is to be done by a female warden and they are not handcuffed when taken for a walk in the yard of the cell. If she is pregnant, the court is required to postpone the date of execution procedure of death sentence. Furthermore the High Court is permitted to commute death sentence to life imprisonment.

The person under death punishment is kept in solitary confinement throughout and all precautions are taken so that he does not commit suicide.

The theory behind all such precautions is that the prisoner must be killed by the State alone as ordained by the judiciary and the society must have its satisfaction of punishing him or her to death.

There is no escape from the dictum: "Since the person is in jail because of the order of the judiciary, the condition of his imprisonment is the continuous responsibility of the judiciary."

Procedure for Hanging

Description and testing of rope:

(1) A Manila rope one inch in diameter shall be used for executions. At least two such ropes in serviceable

condition shall be maintained in every jail where executions are liable to take place. Furthermore, the rope should be 19 feet in length, well twisted, and fully stretched. It should be of equal thickness, capable of passing readily through the noose-ring and sufficiently strong to bear a strain of 280 lbs. with a 7 feet drop.

(2) The ropes shall be tested in the presence of the Superintendent at least a week before the date fixed for the execution and if they fail to pass the test, others shall be obtained at once and tested when received.

(3) Ropes that have been tested shall be locked in a safe place.

(4) On the evening before the execution, the gallows and rope should be examined to ascertain that they have received no injury since being tested.

Furthermore, at least two Manila ropes of serviceable condition shall be kept. Such ropes to be used for hanging are to be tested on two occasions, firstly, at least before a week from the date of execution and secondly on the evening before such execution is to take place. The method of testing such rope is by attaching to one end a sack of sand or clay equal to one and a half times the weight of the prisoner to be executed.

The following scale of drop proportioned to the weight of the prisoner is given for general guidance; the Superintendent must use his discretion and be guided by the advice of the Medical Officer and the physical condition of the prisoner:

For a prisoner under 100 lbs weight 7

For a prisoner under 120 lbs weight 6.

For a prisoner under 140 lbs weight 5-1/2.

For a prisoner under 160 lbs weight 5.

The last figures, namely 7, 6, 5-1/2, 5 denote the height of the drop in terms of feet.

The 'drop' is the length of the rope from a point on the rope opposite the angle of the lower jaw of the criminal as he stands on the scaffold to the point where the rope is embraced in the noose after allowing for the constriction of the neck that takes place in hanging.

Time of the execution:

The time of the execution is specified in early hours of the day. However, the exact time varies according to seasons and is as follows:

November to February	8 a.m.
March, April, September and October	7 a.m.
May to August	6 a.m.

The actual execution process with such background of preparations, etc. has to be carried out in accordance with Paragraphs 868 to 873, which is briefly as follows:

1. The officers required to be present at the execution are the Superintendent and Medical officer of the jail and District Magistrate or a first class magistrate deputed by him.
2. The execution is to be carried out by the public executioner, whenever services of such executioner are available.

If such services are not available, then some trustworthy individual who is locally trained is to be assigned this job. It is the duty of the Superintendent that the person so assigned is competent to fulfil the job.

3. Regulation of the drop: it is the most important factor in deciding the regulation of the death sentence to be executed. The slightest error in deciding the length of

the drop may lead to the lingering death of the condemned man. The drop is regulated according to the height, weight and physical condition of the prisoner. The Superintendent may also take the advice of the Medical Officer in this regard.

The Manual further provides that the Superintendent and Deputy Superintendent will reach the cell of the condemned prisoner and ensure his identity. The warrant of death will be read out to him and the signatures required on various documents such as will etc. may be placed by the prisoner in the presence of the Superintendent. The Superintendent will then move towards the scaffold. In the presence of the Deputy Superintendent, the convict will be pinioned behind his back and his leg irons (if any) will be removed.

The condemned prisoner is then marched to the scaffold under the charge of the Deputy Superintendent. He will be guarded by the Head Warder and six warders, two proceeding in front, two behind and one holding either arm.

After reaching the scaffold, where the Superintendent, the District Magistrate and the Medical Officer are already at their respective places, the warrant should be read out in the vernacular to the convict and he is handed over to the executioner.

The warders holding the arm of the convict shall also mount the scaffold with the convict and place him under the direct beam to which the rope is attached.

The executioner shall next strap his legs tightly together, place the cap over his head and face and adjust the rope tightly around his neck. The noose should be placed one and half inches to the right or left of the middle line and free from the flap of the cap.

The warders holding the condemned man's arms then withdraw and at the signal from the Superintendent, the executioner shall draw the bolt.

The body of such a condemned prisoner should remain suspended for half an hour and shall not be taken down till the medical officer declares life as extinct. The Superintendent is required to return the warrant with an endorsement to the effect that the sentence has been carried out. In India, as it was in UK, there is no provision for a to as certain postmortem of the body, whether the prisoner died instantaneously by breaking of the vertebrae or painfully by strangulation.

The atmosphere in the prison where the person is executed is eerie as during the entire process, all the prisoners are locked in their barracks; more than the condemned prisoner those who witness the execution are uncomfortable. In one case, a District Magistrate told the author that after witnessing a hanging, he could not sleep properly for days and thereafter always deputed a subordinate magistrate to be present at the time of an execution.

□

9

Public Response in India with Diagrams[1]

A Large number of people including judges, lawyers, journalists, women and persons from abroad responded to a Law Commission of India questionnaire on death punishment. A gist of the analysis of replies to the questionnaire, which was contained in the Commission's Report published in 2003, is as follows:

(a) Analysis of Responses from Judges

The Law Commission received responses from judges of different High Courts and subordinate courts to the consultation paper issued by it. Their analysis showed:

(i) Section 354(5) of the Code of Criminal Procedure, 1973 provides that when a person is sentenced to death, the sentence shall be executed by hanging by neck till he is dead. On the question whether this Section 354(5) of the Cr.PC is required to be amended for providing another mode of execution of death sentence, about eighty per cent judges responded in favour of amending it. It means they were of the view that the present mode of execution of death sentence should be changed. Only nineteen per cent judges were satisfied with the present mode. All of the eighty per cent judges who were in favour of amending Section 354(5) suggested that administering lethal injection should be the other mode of execution of death sentence. However, five per cent judges suggested that apart from lethal injection, 'shooting' may also be prescribed as an alternative mode.

(ii) In case another alternative mode of execution of death sentence is provided, question arises whether discretion should be given to the judge or to the convict to select the mode of execution of death sentence. Forty-five per cent judges opined that discretion should be given to the convict and thirty-six per cent judges were of the view that discretion should be given to the judge in choosing the mode of execution of death sentence.

(iii) Regarding whether there should be statutory right to appeal to the Supreme Court even when the High Court had confirmed death punishment, ninety-two per cent of the judges opined that appeal by way of right should be provided against the judgement of the High Court.

(iv) On the question whether there should be a bench of not less than five judges in the Supreme Court to hear and decide cases relating to death sentence, fifty-one per cent of the judges answered in the negative, while forty-nine per cent judges were of the view that cases relating to death sentence should be heard and decided by a bench of not less than five judges. Among them, thirty-three per cent were of the view that the rule of majority should be applicable. Of these thirty-three per cent, six per cent judges were in favour of applying the rule of two-third majority. Three per cent judges suggested that the rule of unanimity should be applied. It is relevant to note that District Judges of all districts in Uttar Pradesh, which is the biggest State in India, sent their responses.

(b) Analysis of the Responses from Persons other than Judges

A large number of responses from general public, persons from the legal profession, doctors, officers of the armed forces and police officers including those from the Central Bureau of Investigation (CBI) which is like the Federal Bureau of Investigation (FBI) of the United States of America were received. Their responses are as follows:

(i) As regards Section 354(5) of the Code of Criminal Procedure, 1973, about eighty-nine per cent persons were in favour of an amendment providing for other modes of execution of death sentence. However, eleven per cent of the respondents persons did not suggest amendment to this section. Seventy-three per cent of those who were in favour of providing other modes of execution of death sentence preferred that administering lethal injection should be an alternative method of execution of death sentence. While ten per cent preferred using electric chair, five per cent preferred shooting by firing squad as an alternative mode of execution death sentence.

(ii) Fifty one per cent of those who were in favour of retaining the present mode of execution of death sentence, i.e. 'hanging by neck till death', were of the view that the execution should be done in a public place. But forty-nine per cent persons said that hanging should be done at a private place like a jail.

(iii) On the question whether discretion should be given to the court for choosing the mode of execution of death sentence, sixty-two per cent answered in the negative and thirty-eight per cent were in its favour. Eighty-three per cent persons in their responses opined that there should be a statutory right to appeal to the Supreme Court in cases where the death sentence awarded by the trial court and confirmed by the High Court. However, seventeen per cent were not in favour of providing a right of appeal to the Supreme Court in such cases.

(iv) Ninety-nine per cent persons were of the view that in the Supreme Court, cases relating to death sentence should be heard and decided by a bench of not less than five judges. Among them, forty-seven per cent were in favour of applying a rule of simple majority and thirty-three per cent were in favour of the rule of two-third majority. Twenty per cent were in favour of the rule of unanimity.

The Law Commission also held a seminar on the question of execution of death punishment but the opinion expressed in the seminar cannot be said to be representative of the public opinion at large because only a few people expressed their opinion, although it was attended by lawyers, law students, journalists, officers of the armed forces, and the police, including the then Director (chief) of the Central Bureau of Investigation, S.K. Sharma.

Surprisingly, lawyers and law students preferred hanging over lethal injection. From the police personnel and law students, some favoured public hanging as against private hanging in jail to create greater deterrent. But there was unanimity that there should be right of appeal to the Supreme Court. Those who wanted right of appeal to the Supreme Court were, however, divided regarding the constitution of the bench, whether it should consist of three or five judges and whether the verdict should be by unanimity or simple majority.

Members of the armed forces, however, stressed that there should be no appeal to the Supreme Court against the punishment provided by a Court Martial as the verdict was confirmed by the higher authorities in the concerned branch of the armed forces as well as Ministry of Defence and they had the power to mitigate the sentence.

It may be mentioned that the *Times of India* on July 27, 2003 also conducted an SMS poll asking the question "Are public executions the best punishment for heinous crimes?" The response was sixty-nine per cent 'Yes' and thirty-one per cent 'No'.

Do you want amendment of Section 354(5) of the Code of Criminal Procedure which provides "When any person is sentenced to death, the sentence shall direct that he be hanged by the neck till he is dead"

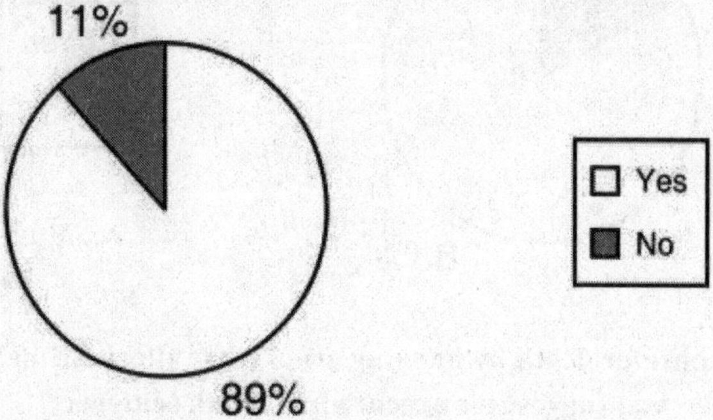

If you want hanging to remain, do you prefer hanging in public or in private as a mode of execution

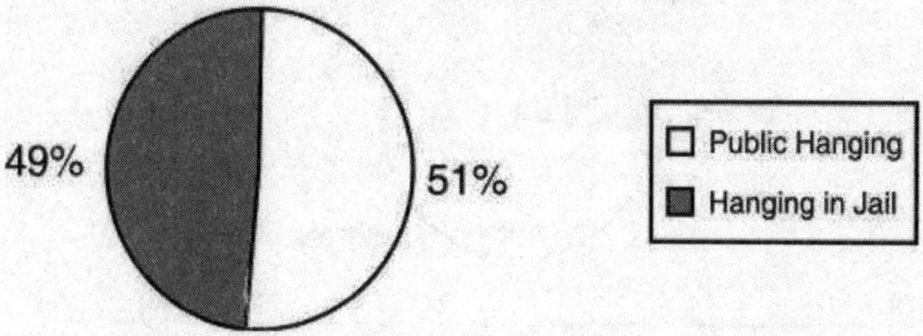

Should the discretion on the mode of execution be given to the convict?

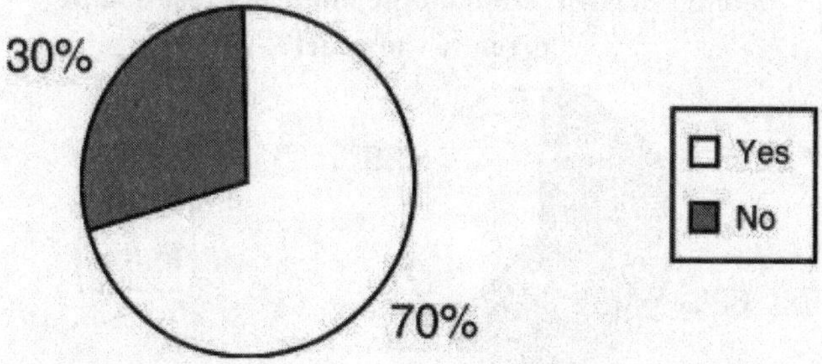

Should a right of appeal to Supreme Court be given?

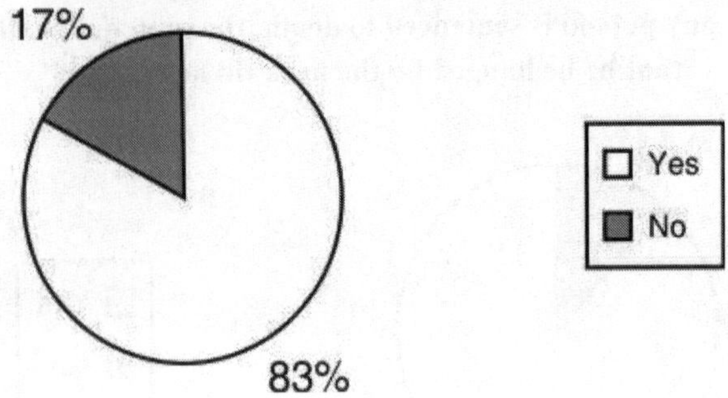

If you consider death by hanging cruel what alternate method do you suggest for execution of death sentence?

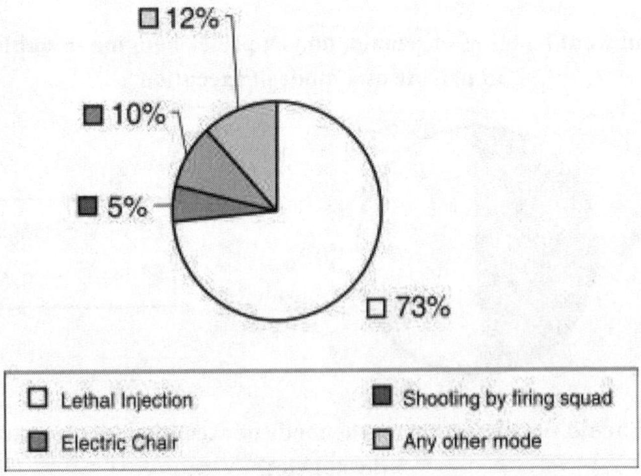

Should the discretion on the mode of execution be given to the court?

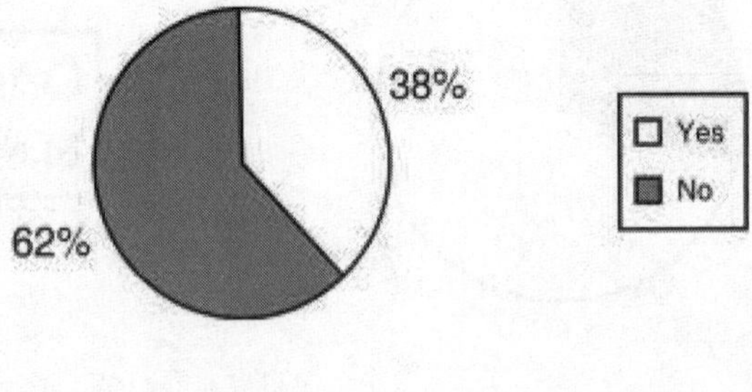

Decision on death sentence should be by 5-Judge Bench of Supreme Court?

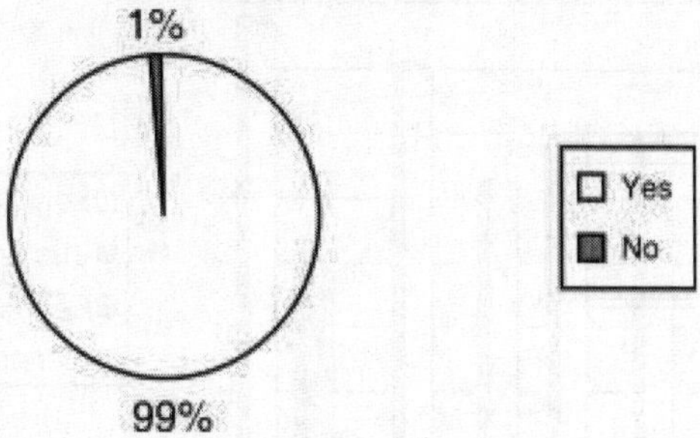

What should be the voting requirement of the Supreme Court Bench hearing death sentence cases?

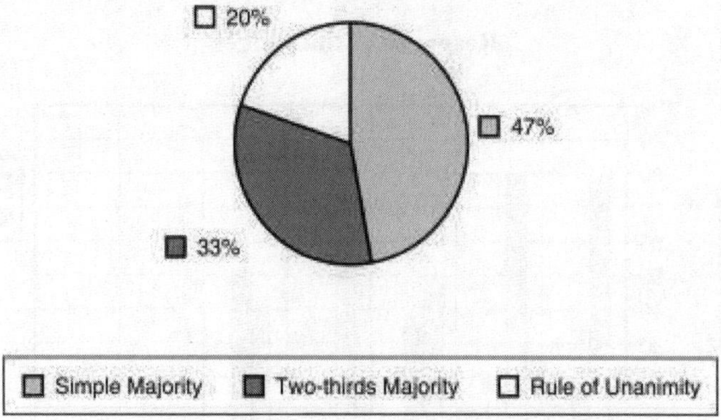

Lethal Injection Participants Type

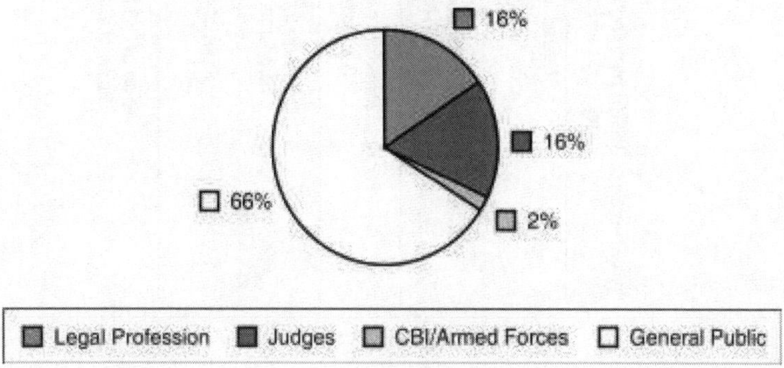

Category wise breakup of participants in the questionnaire

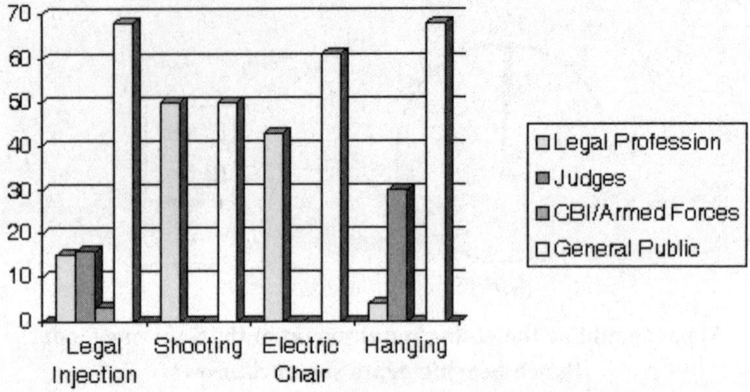

Response of the Judges

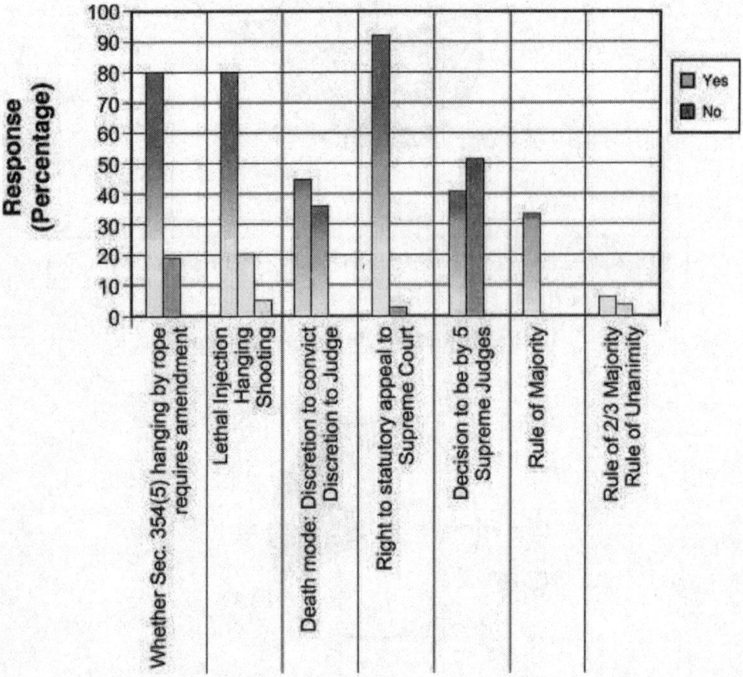

Summing Up of the Indian Position

As far as India is concerned, the public reaction at present is against the trend of humanising the mode of execution of death punishment. It is peculiar, yet understandable. This is because the general public is in favour of an archaic and cruel form of carrying out the death punishment, such as hanging. The fact that a substantial number of people feel it should be done in public is because of the very low conviction rate, which is only about six per cent, and the increasing crime rate in India. The rise of terrorism with increasing victimization of innocent people is also one of the main reasons for this attitude amongst Indians. In addition, investigation and judicial agencies are not able to bring the actual persons who commit crimes before the courts of justice. The general public feels that today the high, the rich and the mighty are able to manage delays, tamper with witnesses and are able to abuse the system and go scot-free.

If crimes in India are to be reduced, there is a pressing need of bringing the offender to quick justice. He must know that he will be punished immediately which will have a deterrent effect. Otherwise crime would continue to plague the country at an intolerable rate. To check this, there is a pressing need to change the criminal procedure. Furthermore, the judges instead of being mute spectators in criminal trials should take an active part in finding the truth, as in France, such as questioning the prosecution as to why vital witnesses are dropped and instead of passing strictures against the faults of prosecutors, find those who are at fault and initiate criminal prosecution accompanied by severe punishment.

Besides, the old rule that a guilty person has the right to remain silent during trial and the entire burden of proving the guilt rests on the prosecution should be given up. For example, if the accused fails to answer questions put to him by the judge, the latter should be free to draw an adverse inference against the accused. Moreover, if the dictum that the person is innocent till proven guilty is to have any meaning and ninety-nine guilty persons may go scot-free but one innocent should not be punished, one should also ask why the ninety-nine who have committed crimes have gone scot-free. These changes in law would make people more law-abiding. Also, law should provide for more stringent and quick punishment for economic offences like in the United States of America. For example, B. Ramalinga Raju, owner of giant computer company Satyam, confessed his guilt in India, though he was also wanted for fraud in the USA because while in India, he would get seven years of jail, in the USA he would have got sixty years.

In view of the personal psychology of a judge, as in other human beings, and constitution of benches of higher judiciary with different judges, I personally feel that Justice Bhagwati's observation in his dissenting judgement in *Bachan Singh's* case that arbitrariness is unfortunately inbuilt in the higher judiciary whether a person should die or live is a lottery. Justice Bhagwati's observation that the full bench of the Supreme Court should decide a death punishment case is very relevant. Furthermore it should be decided by unanimity and not majority because it is irreversible and irrevocable if an error is committed. There are, as has been seen, cases of innocents being executed in the United States and the United Kingdom. Similarly, since the decision of the Supreme Court being the law binding on all courts under Article 41 of the Constitution, it will help them in determining discretion on the question of death punishment. At present, for example, there is no unanimity in the Supreme Court as to how many years a person spending in the death row constitutes the mitigating circumstance for comuitting death sentence to life imprisonment. Also there is no settled rule whether a juvenile or mentally retarded person should be given death punishment or not.

The full bench of the Supreme Court should decide cases of death punishment because they are few as compared to the United States. And there also, a bench of nine judges decides such cases, though by majority. Moreover, if the full bench of the Supreme Court can hear property matters, should this not apply to much graver issues like death punishment? If the Supreme Court of India can constitute a full bench to decide cases regarding property like the *Golaknath's* case, the *Privy Purses* case, *the Bank Nationalisation* case, or the *Kesavananda Bharti* case, does a decision on a matter of life and death not deserve consideration by the full bench of the Supreme Court? Otherwise, India would be blamed for weighing property with a golden scale and life with a butcher's scale.

Also the Supreme Court should not have the *suo-motu* power to enhance punishment from life to death as the accused is robbed of any appeal on such a vital question, which I emphasise again because of the qualitative difference from all other punishments, as it is irreversible if afterwards it is found that an error had been committed in awarding the death punishment.

Lastly, as has been emphasised earlier, if death punishment is to be continued, judges have a special responsibility that the life should be extinguished as painlessly and as quickly as possible and without mutilation of the body. Apart from the fact that hanging has become an archaic method, even the Law Commission of India had recommended lethal injection in its 187th Report of 2003. Even electrocution as a method of executing death punishment has been given up by many States in the United States, and the Nebraska Supreme Court struck it down even though it was the only method in the State. Therefore, it is submitted that the Supreme Court can strike down Section 554(5) of the Criminal Procedure Code of 1973 when a death punishment case comes before the Supreme Court or take this issue as a public interest litigation *suo-motu*.

It is high time Parliament itself examines this question and substitutes hanging by lethal injection which at present is the most humane method of executing death sentence. Also the law should provide for post-mortem of the body as is required in America and in the United Kingdom before it abolished death punishment. Similarly, just as a choice of method of execution is given to the inmate in America, it would be better if a choice is given to the accused as is done in case of Courts Martial which give the death punishment by shooting or hanging. However, those members of the judiciary and Parliament who think that the present law of death punishment by hanging is not barbaric should witness a hanging themselves.

As pointed out earlier, there being no settled question regarding imposition of death punishment on juveniles and in *Roper* vs. *Simmons* the United States Supreme Court declared it unconstitutional. India should introduce a law banning death punishment for juveniles to those who were under 18 years at the time of committing an offence, and also on pregnant women as she has to take care of an infant. It may be remembered that the United Kingdom as early as 1908 barred the killing of children under the age of 16, and raised the age to 18 in 1933. Also there is a law on complete prohibition of hanging pregnant women from 1931. Similarly mental retarded convicts should not be given death punishment by law.

Finally, the President of India and the Governor of the States under Articles 74 and 164 of the Constitution of India are given powers to pardon or commute sentences given by courts. But no time limit has been prescribed within which the mercy petitions have to be decided. Since expeditious disposal of cases is now a fundamental right, it is necessary to enact a law fixing a time limit for disposing of mercy petition.

□

10

Conclusion

There is a growing trend in the world towards abolishing death sentence. As many as 97 countries have already abolished it except for crimes which involve the security of the country. Gamong is the only country which has abolished it for all offences. Death punishment, however is valid in 57 countries. Although the countries with death punishment on their statute books is less, 60% of the world's population lives in these countries as the most populous countries like China, India, Russia and the United States of America have not abolished death punishment. It is equally significant that the capital sentence exists in industrial democracies, viz. India, Israel, Japan, Singapore, South Korea and the United States of America.

With the march of civilisation, torturous and gruesome methods of extinguishing life like burning at the stake, breaking the person on a wheel, strangulation and garotte, beheading and guillotine have become non-existent except in some Middle-Eastern countries like Iran and Saudi Arabia where stoning to death or beheading is still practised. Similarly, in these and a few Islamic countries, 'crimes' like adultery or changing one's religion besides murder are also subjected to death punishment. In most countries, death punishment is now restricted to aggravated, pre-meditated and gruesome murder. However, with the rise of narcotic trafficking and instances of terrorism, there is a growing trend of including these offences in the category of capital punishment, as has been done by Pakitsan which reintroduced capital punishment after the terrorist killing of school children in Peshawar in late 2014.

In the United States, 15 States do not have capital punishment and other States which have it are employing more and more humane methods of extinguishing life. Hanging, because it often results in agonising death by strangulation, has been given up by all States in the US, except Delaware, New Hampshire and Washington. But there also the inmate can choose another method. Electrocution, which was popular in the United States in the twentieth century, is also on its way out and now lethal injection, which first makes the inmate unconscious and then poisonous substance is injected so that he dies in his sleep and results in no mutilation of the body, is becoming more acceptable in most States in the US which still retain the capital sentence.

The State Supreme Courts as well as the Federal Supreme Court in America have done commendable service in the sphere of imposing capital punishment. The Supreme Court of Nebraska in 2008 struck down electrocution as a cruel and unusual punishment, although there was no other method of capital punishment. As a result, all executions were stayed till the state legislature introduced lethal injection in 2011. Similarly, the Supreme Courts of Massachusetts and New York have also struck down electrocution. Moreover, in 1972 the *Furman* case upheld the validity of death punishment as not cruel and unusual under the Eighth Amendment of the US Constitution, but invalidated the procedure adopted by the States as arbitrary. As a result all executions were stayed. Subsequently, as mentioned earlier, laws which did not give discretion but mandated the judiciary to impose death punishment were struck down. It also contributed to decreasing the offences marked for capital punishment such as rape even of minors unless it was accompanied by murder. Moreover, the US Supreme Court held that mentally retarded persons who have an I.Q. of less than 70 and juveniles below the age of 18 at the time of commission of crime could not be given death punishment. In coming to these conclusions, the Supreme Court followed a novel practice of weighing public opinion as expressed by the majority of state legislatures, and in 2005, it also invalidated death penalty for juveniles following the world trend and the UN resolution, although its own government voted against it.

Although the majority in liberal democracies like the United States of America and India are for retaining capital punishment, it is universally true that capital punishment is awarded to those who have no capital, are illiterate and belong the minority communities, for example, blacks in America; in other parts of the world, it is inflicted 'on others'. It is also proved that it is not a deterrent and murders continue. If the statistics in the US are any indication, they reveal that the murder rate in the States which have capital sentence is more than those States which do not.

The Supreme Court of India, as seen earlier, has retained hanging as a mode of extinguishing life, saying that it is practised in 'most countries'. This, however, is not correct. Secondly, when it was demonstrated that hanging was an archaic method, it should have struck it down as unconstitutional and violative of a fair, just and reasonable procedure as the State of Nebraska in the United States subsequently did. Instead, it lamely justified the decision of the larger Constitution Bench in *Bachan Singh's* case having upheld it and that Article 21 provides for it. In *Deena's* case, challenge was to the method of hanging provided by the one and a half century old procedure as contained in Section 354(5) of the Criminal Procedure Code. If this method was given up, there would be no way to carry out death punishment. Hence, the Supreme Court upheld death punishment as it said it was not empowered to legislate. This reasoning is hardly logical as mentioned earlier.

It may be mentioned that in India, there is no post-mortem of the inmate, as was the case in England and in States in the US where hanging was practised, to find out if the person died by strangulation or breaking of the spinal cord. It may also be mentioned that in the US, regardless of the method by which death punishment is carried out, post-mortem is required to be held. This should be done in India too.

All over the world, where death punishment is imposed, it is done privately inside the prison walls. In the US, however, besides officials, relatives, close friends and media without cameras are allowed to witness an execution. In India, this is not done and the Supreme Court dismissed the public interest litigation of the media to witness and televise the execution of Satwant Singh and Kehar Singh, who were sentenced to death for the assassination of former Prime Minister Indira Gandhi.

Nonetheless, George W. Bush, Jr. after arresting Saddam Hussain, the President of Iraq, not only decided to hang him to death publicly, but also allowed the world's media to witness the gory spectacle, and televise it worldwide. It was an abominal decision. Besides, outraging humanity, it firmed the Iraqis' resolve to fight the Americans till American finally withdrew from their country.

Since the birth of nation-states, with people living in geographically defined countries or empires, the threat to peace has emerged from countries. The United Nations was created for the peaceful settlement of disputes between countries. Post-World War II and the emergence of rival Cold War blocs led by the United States and the Soviet Union, with their nuclear weapons, world peace was threatened by them and subsequently by nuclear armed China and recently by North Korea. With India, Pakistan, Iran and Israel acquiring nuclear capability, maintaining regional peace has acquired importance.

But the rise of terrorism has created altogether new problems. Terrorist organisations and their leaders are not wedded to any one country, but find supporters across national borders. They pose a serious threat to the world and regional peace with the ability to obtain all sorts of arms, including weapons of mass destruction. This situation raises new complications to peace. The United Nations, the main peace-keeping body, is designed to avoid war between nations. It only recognises countries and not any group as its members. It does not have a negotiating forum for arms control or disarmament to ensure world peace threatened by individual terrorist groups. Secondly, the countries threatened by them also do not have any organised mechanism to negotiate with individual groups which threaten peace in the world or regions. Finally, the capability of these groups of people to obtain all sorts of weapons including weapons of mass destruction, such as nuclear warheads, bacteriological and chemical weapons in spite of international conventions to ban the use of the latter two types of weapons, is a grave threat. The nation-states as well as the United Nations need to tackle this situation on priority basis with necessary organisational changes. If they do not act swiftly, all their efforts and treaties in the sphere of disarmament, arms control and confidence building would come to a naught, and humanity may be engulfed in uncontrollable anarchy. To this end, the problem of international terrorism, which is the most serious issue threatening world peace, needs to be tackled urgently by all nations.

□

End Notes

Chapter 2

Medieval Methods of Execution of Death Punishment

1. See 187 Report of the Law Commission of India 2003 (New Delhi: Ministry of Law & Justice 2003); and 'Top 10 Gruesome Methods of Execution,' http://listverse. com/2007/09/12. Accessed on 07.08.11.
2. http://www.fotosearch.com/photos-images/christ-crucified. html. Accessed on 11.11.11.
3. http://photobucket.com/images/burned%20at%20the%20stake/ Accessed on 11.11.11.
4. http://en.wikipedia.org/wiki/Breaking_wheel Accessed on 11.11.11.
5. http://boisdejustice.com/ Accessed on 11.11.11.
6. 187th report of the Law Commission of India, 2003, *loc. cit.*
7. *Ibid.*
8. The history of beheading and decapitation www.capitalpunishmentuk.org/behead.html
9. This summary is made from the book by, Evelyn Anthony, *Charles the King* (London: Coronet Books, Hodder and Stoughton, 1961). Also see Execution of Charles I.

   Also see Trial and Execution of Charles I with picture; http://en.wikipedia.org/wiki/Charles-I of England Accessed on 06.08.11.
10. http://en.wikipedia.org/wiki/Garrote. Accessed on 8.8.2011.

Chapter 3

Present Methods of Execution of Death Punishment

1. See 187 Report of the Law Commission of India, 2003, New Delhi: Ministry of Law & Justice 2003. Also see 10 methods of Capital Punishments in the World — Infofpelese; Types of Execution — Microsoft Internet Explorer. Types of Execution Illustrated Guide — An Illustrated Guide to Eight Types of Methods of Execution — Microsoft interim Explorer. http://en.wikipedia.org/wiki/Execution by firing squad. Accessed on 8.8.2011.
2. http://www.google.co.in/#hl=mr&gs_nf=1&cp=8&gs_id=n&xhr=t&q=Firing+Squad&pf=p&sclient=psyab&oq=Firing+S&aq=0L&aqi=g-L4&aql=&gs_sm=&gs_upl=&gs_l=&pbx=1&bav=on.2,or.r_gc.r_pw.r_qf.,cf.osb&fp=cc9ae866b3c2ade8&biw=819&bih=452. Accessed on 8.8.2011.
3. http://www.dreamstime.com/stock-photos-hanging-noose-image3832533. Accessed on 10.8.2011.
4. http://www.clarkprosecutor.org/html/death/methods.htm. Accessed on 10.8.2011. Also see p. 160-166.
5. George Orwell, renowned for his novels *Animal Farm* (1945) and *Nineteen Eighty-four* (1949), was one of the most notable political writers and literary journalists of the twentieth century. From 1922 to 1927, he served in Burma (now the Union of Myanmar) as a member of the Indian Imperial Police. Out of that experience came this classic essay. 'A Hanging.' George Orwell — Hanging — Essay, Microsoft Explorer. http://www.k-1.com/Orwell site/work/essays/hanging.html. Accessed on 10.8.2011.
6. http://en.wikipedia.org/wiki/Timothy_Evans. Accessed on 16.8.2011.
7. Timothy Evans — Wikpedia Encyclopedia Internet Explorer. *Ibid.* Accessed on 16.8.2011.
8. http://www.clarkprosecutor.org/html/death/methods.htm. Accessed on 18.8.2011.

9. http://listverse.com/2007/09/18/top-10-modern-methods-of-execution/. Accessed on 18.8.2011.
10. The story of the last days of Rosenbergs and the photograph therein are taken from Louis Nizer, *Implosion Conspiracy* (New York 1972). Alvin H. Goldstine, *The Unequalled Death of Julius and Ethel Rosenberg* (New York: Lawrence Hill & Co., 1975). Also see Julius and Ethel Rosenberg execution and trial — http://en.wikipedia.org/wiki/ Julius_and_Ethel_ Rosenberg-Wikpedia; Rosenberg Trial — Cold War Museum — http://www.coldwar.org/ —Wikpedia. Accessed on 18.8.2011.
11. http://en.wikipedia.org/wiki/Julius_and_Ethel_Rosenberg. Accessed on 18.8.2011.
12. *For photographs, see Elvin H. Goldstein, The Unquie Death of Julius and Ethel Rosenberg; from the following sources: Sunset at Sing Sing: UPI Rosenberg supporters at 17th Street, NYC: UPI, Washington D.C., 1975.*
13. *Ibid.*
14. *Ibid.*
15. *Ibid.*
16. Ivan Solotaroff, *The Last Face You'll Ever See: The Private Life of the American Death Penalty*, New York, Harper Collins, Inc., 2001.
17. *http://www.google.co.in/#hl=mr&output=search&sclient=psy-ab&q=sanctioned+the+fund+through+the+Corporation+of+Public+Broadcasting+for+recrimination+of+the+case&oq.* Accessed on 20.8.2011.
18. Louis Nizer, *Implosion Conspiracy* (New York 1972).
19. http://www.clarkprosecutor.org/html/death/methods.htm. Accessed on 18.8.2011.
20. http://www.google.co.in/#hl=mr&sclient=psy-ab&q=Evans. Accessed on 18.8.2011.
21. http://www.clarkprosecutor.org/html/death/methods.htm. Accessed on 18.8.2011.
22. *Ibid.*
23. *The Indian Express*, September 23, 2011, p. 13.
24. http://lawcommissionofindia.nic.in/cpds1.pdf.

Chapter 4
Situation of Death Penalty and Moratorium in the World

1. Use of Capital Punishment in the World — Countrywise — Wikipedia; Capital Punishment — Wikipedia, finsce Encyclopedia. Maps figures and statics are taken from this source. http://en.wikipedia.org/wiki/Use of capital punishment by country Accessed on 24.8.2011.
2. http://en.wikipedia.org/wiki/File:Death_Penalty_World_Map.png Accessed on 24.8.2011.
3. http://en.wikipedia.org/wiki/UN_moratorium_on_the_death_penalty Accessed on 24.8.2011.
4. *Ibid.*
5. http://en.wikipedia.org/wiki/Capital_punishment#Execution_for_drug-related_offences Accessed on 25.8.2011.
6. http://www.infoplease.com/ipa/A0777460.html Accessed on 25.8.2011.
7. http://en.wikipedia.org/wiki/Use_of_capital_punishment_by_country Accessed on 26.8.2011.
8. *Ibid.*

Chapter 5
Situation and Methods of Death Punishment in the United States of America

1. For map, statistics and material in this chapter, see Death Punishment in the United States — Microsoft Explorer, Public Opinion, Harris Polls, Gallup Polls, up to date since 2008; also see Capital Punishment in the United States, — Wikipedia. http://www.religioustolerance.org executh.htm. Accessed on 27.08.2011.
2. http://en.wikipedia.org/wiki/Capital_punishment_in_the_United_States.
3. http://www.clarkprosecutor.org/html/death/methods.htm.
4. http://www.google.co.in/#hl=mr&sclient=psy-ab&q=Illinois abolished death penalty in the year 2009.
5. http://www.google.co.in/#hl=mr&sclient=psy-ab&q=choice to inmates as to the method of execution.

6. http://www.gallup.com/poll/151460/record-rate-honesty-ethics-members-congress-low.aspx;:https://www.prisonlegalnews.org/.../22841_display Article.aspx.
7. http://www.gallup.com/poll/1606/death-penalty.aspx.
8. http://wiki.answers.com/Q/What_are_the_three_levels_of_the_US_federal_court_system.
9. http://en.wikipedia.org/wiki/Capital_punishment_in_the_United_States.
10. *Ibid.*
11. *Ibid.*
12. *Ibid.*
13. *Ibid.*
14. *Furman* vs. *Georgia* 408 US 238 (1972).
15. *Gregg* vs. *Georgia* 428 US 153.
16. *Atkins* vs. *Virginia*, 536 US 304 (2002).
17. *Roper* vs. *Simmons*, 543 US 551 (2005).

Chapter 6
Death Penalty in India and Modes of Execution of Death Sentence

1. *Mithu etc.* vs. *State of Punjab*, etc. 1983(2)SCC277 Supreme Court of United States has done, as seen earlier. However, as far as a pregnant woman is concerned, she, in India as in the United States, can be executed after delivery.
2. *Bachan Singh* vs. *State of Punjab*, 1980 (2) SCC 684 and for minority judgement 1982 *(3)SCC 24.*
3. *Machi Singh and Ors.* vs. *State of Punjab*, 1983 (2) SCC473.
4. *Deena alias Deen Dayal and Ors. Etc.* vs. *UOI and Ors.* etc. 1983(4) SCC645.
5. *Ibid.*
6. *Bachan Singh etc.* vs. *State of Punjab etc.* 1982(3)SCC24.
7. This issue from Law Commission's 35th Report on Capital Punishment 1967 has already been dealt with in the Introduction.
8. Bill No. VII, introduced in Rajya Sabha on April 30, 1987 and debated on March 11 and 25, 1988; Edited by Dr. N.M. Ghatate,

Atal Bihari Vajpayee: A Constructive Parliamentarian (New Delhi: Ocean Books Pvt. Ltd., 2012), pp. 121-33.

9. Sections 34 and 37 of the Army Act and the Air Force Act of 1950 and Sections 34, 37-39, 42, 48 and 52 of the Navy Act of 1957. Note: *paragraphs (a) to (q) are applicable to all Acts, while (r) to (t) to Air Force Act and (v) to Navy Act.*
10. *Prithi Singh Bedi* etc. vs. *UOI and Ors.*, 1982(2)SCC1413.
11. 187th Report of the Law Commission of India, 2003.
12. *Ibid.*
13. Constitution of Armed Forces Appellate Tribunal was recommended by the Law Commission of India in its 169th Report of 1999. This report was accepted and the Armed Forces Tribunal Act of 1907 came into force in 2008.
14. The 44th Constitutional Amendment of 1969 provided more safeguards to the detenus and amended clauses (4) to (7) but this Amendment has not yet been brought into force despite the observations of the Supreme Court in *A.K. Roy etc.* vs. *UOI*, SCC(4)326. Also see Dr. N.M. Ghatate, *Emergency, Constitution & Democracy* (New Delhi, Shipra Publications, 2008).

Chapter 7

Appeal Procedure in Cases of Death Penalty

1. See Sections 121, 130, 132, 302, 30-07. Section 303 was declared unconstitutional vide *Mithu* vs. *State of Punjab*, 1982 (2) SCC 277.
2. Prof. *A.R. Black Shield:* 'Capital Punishment in India,' Vol. 2. *The Journal of Indian Law Institute,* p.137, 1979.
3. *Bachan Singh* etc. vs. *State of Punjab* 198 (3) SCC 24.
4. *E.K. Chandrashekhar* vs. *State of Kerala*, 1955(2) SCC 99.
5. *Harbans Singh*, 1982(2) SCC 101.
6. *State of U.P.* vs. *Suman Dass*, 1972(3) SCC 201.
7. *Raghubir Singh* vs. *State of Haryana*, 1975(3) SCC 37.
8. *Gurudas Singh* vs. *State of Rajasthan*, 1975(4) SCC 490.
9. *Bhawan Swaroop* vs. *State of U.P.*, 1971(3) SCC 759.
10. *Ragho Mai* vs. *State of U.P.*, 1976(4) SCC 297.

11. *Babu* vs. *State of U.P.*, 1965(2) SCC 771.
12. *Masalti* vs. *State of U.P.*, 1964(4) SCC 133.
13. *Gurucharan Singh* vs. *State of Punjab*, 1963(3) SCC 585.
14. *Mukhtiar Singh* vs. *State of Punjab*, 1972(4) SC 834.
15. *Kehar Singh* vs. *State (Delhi Administration)*, 1983(3) SCC 609.
16. *Ediga Anamma* vs. *State of A.P.*, 1974 (4) SC 443.
17. *Bhoor Singh* vs. *State of Punjab*, 1974(4) SCC 754.
18. *Gurudas Singh* vs. *State of Rajasthan*, 1975(4) SCC 490.
19. *Raghubir Singh* vs. *State of Hayrana*, 1975(3) SCC 37.
20. *Bharwad Mepa* vs. *State of Bombay*, 1960(2) SCC 172.
21. *Dhananjoy Chatterjee alias Dhana* vs. *State of West Bengal*, 1994(2) SCC 220.
22. *Yogendra Morarji* vs. *State of Gujarat*, 1980(2) SCC 218.
23. *Chandra Mohan Tiwari* vs. *State of MP*, 1992(2) SCC 105.
24. *Nadir Khan* vs. *The State (Delhi Admn.)*, 1975(2) SCC 406.
25. *Sahib Singh* vs. *State of Haryana*, 1990(2) SCC 385.
26. *Surjit Singh* vs. *State of Punjab*, 1984 Supp SCC 518.

Chapter 8
Execution Procedure of Death Sentence in India

1. Details of the procedure for execution of death punishment in India are the same in every State as described in the *Jail Manual of Punjab & Haryana, 1988* (Chandigarh: Govt. Printing Press, 1988).

Chapter 9
Public Response in India with Diagrams

1. The contents of this Chapter are extracted from the 187th Report of The Law Commission of India, 2003 (New Delhi: Ministry of Law & Justice, Government of India.)

□

Index

F

G

H

I

S

□□□